The End of Law?

The End of Law?

TIMOTHY O'HAGAN

Basil Blackwell

First published in 1984 by
Basil Blackwell Publishers Ltd.,
108 Cowley Road, Oxford OX4 1JF, UK.

British Library Cataloguing in Publication Data

O'Hagan, Timothy
The end of law?
1. Sociological jurisprudence
I. Title
340'115 K370

ISBN 0-631-14535-4 Pbk

Typeset by Freeman Graphics, Tonbridge
Printed and bound in Great Britain by
Billing & Sons, Worcester

Contents

Introduction 1

1 The 'New' Radicalism in Jurisprudence 4
1.1 The left critique 5
1.2 The right critique 21
Notes 27

2 Kant and Hegel 31
2.1 Kant: an unhappy compromise 31
2.2 Hegel and the law: the problem of mediations 35
Notes 44

3 Marxism and the *Rechtsstaat* 46
3.1 Marx's flirtation with *Gemeinschaftlichkeit* 46
3.2 A Marxist theory of law? 53
3.3 The 'rational kernel' of Marxist historicism 65
Notes 81

4 Tönnies and After 86
4.1 Tönnies and the formalization of the *Gemeinschaft/Gesellschaft* distinction 86
4.2 Pashukanis: law as an expression of exchange relations 90
4.3 Kamenka and Tay: 'bureaucratic-administrative regulation' 93
Notes 96

5 Experiments of Living 99
5.1 Libertarianism and pluralism 99
5.2 J. S. Mill's three formulae 100
5.3 J. S. Mill and the law 102
5.4 The social construction of privacy and harm 105
5.5 Enforcing the *Gemeinschaft:* Lord Devlin 111
Notes 114

6 Towards a *Rechtsstaat* 116
6.1 *Rechtsstaat* and despotism 116
6.2 Law and legitimacy 120
6.3 The law and the *Rechtsstaat* 131
6.4 Substantive rights 143
6.5 Degrees of relativism 150
Notes 157

Bibliography 170

Index 181

Acknowledgements

My main debt is to my former colleague and collaborator in jurisprudence teaching, Jean-Marie Chandelle, from whom I have learnt much about the matters discussed in this book.

My thanks go to Nikki Rankin for research assistance. The Alexander von Humboldt Foundation financed a stay at the University of Konstanz in the summer of 1982, when a first draft of the book was written. I wish to thank the Foundation for its support and members of the Konstanz Philosophy Department for their hospitality. In particular I should like to thank Albrecht Wellmer for detailed help and criticism.

Harvester Press has granted permission to use in section 3.3 material first published in 1981 in D-H. Ruben and J. Mepham (eds.), *Issues in Marxist Philosophy*, volume 4; M. Warnock has granted permission for quotes from J. S. Mill; and Oxford University Press for H. L. A. Hart's *The Concept of the Law*.

Acknowledgements

Introduction

The End of Law? engages in some bridge-building between three disciplines which have been pursued for the most part in isolation from one another: first, contemporary Anglo-American jurisprudence represented by Hart and Dworkin; second, the classics of social theory in the texts of Kant, Hegel, Marx, Mill and some of their successors; third, the detailed work of civil liberties campaigners, which has revealed how imperfectly the ideal type of constitutional order is embodied in empirical reality. I address myself to texts in jurisprudence and social theory directly, using them as primary sources. Questions of civil liberties I approach through secondary sources, in particular the excellent work of Hewitt, Beddard and Young, which I have plundered wholesale, with the aim, it is hoped, of reinforcing their conclusions and locating them in a broader theoretical context.

The book also mounts a polemic against two critical schools of thought in recent jurisprudence, both hostile to properties of the legal systems of advanced capitalist states, in particular to their alleged formalism, abstraction and distance from the people to whom they are addressed. For the left critique, it is in virtue of these properties that our legal systems have been able to enforce, perpetuate and disguise the relations of class exploitation embodied by capitalism. For the right critique, it is in virtue of these very same properties, viewed from the opposed political perspective, that a new form of life is emerging, in which individuals and groups within society assert their rights and challenge the established political order in an unacceptable fashion; they also allow for progressive, programmatic legislation, designed to make real and universal certain fundamental rights in forms which are alleged to be unacceptable to ordinary people.

I trace the genealogy of these schools through some selective intellectual history, showing how the idea of the *Rechtsstaat*, the universe of individual citizens, legally free and equal, inaugurated by capitalism, was received by Kant, Hegel and Marx. My purpose here is both expository and critical. I am concerned both with the historical context of these classics and with the rational kernel that can be extracted from them for use in our own jurisprudence. I follow this intellectual history through to the works of Tönnies and Pashukanis and examine them in the light of Kamenka's and Tay's typology of forms of legal order. I invoke Mill's classic exposition of libertarian pluralism, the *Essay on Liberty*, as a model which is both desirable and attainable, though only when certain material and ideological conditions are realized: most importantly, when the means of exercising freedom are more equally distributed between classes and individuals. I go beyond Mill in arguing that a system of rights can be understood and defended as a solution to the problem posed by a particular stage of social evolution, which is to find a form of autonomous, non-manipulated social intercourse for citizens of a technologically advanced state.

I conclude by considering ways in which those conditions may be more or less successfully realized. Mill and Dworkin have warned of the danger of the 'tyranny of the majority', the infringement of the rights of individuals and minority groups, inscribed in the process of democracy. But that warning should not be misread. It does not mean, *pace* Isaiah Berlin, that the democrats' goal of redistributing power on a more egalitarian basis is incompatible with the libertarians' goal of defending civil rights, or that the latter goal is likely to be better served by despotism than by democracy. It means simply that the democratic process does not in itself guarantee civil rights unless it is controlled by self-imposed constitutional restraints. In the present situation, where there is little popular control over agents of government and little popular access to the information on which state power rests, where there is also only fragile protection of citizens' rights against that power, the two struggles, for democracy and for civil rights, come together.

But, beyond the conjunctural convergence of the two

struggles, if my critical polemic against both left and right utopians is correct, we should also look for a continuation of the two processes in any future order. The search for the withering-away of the *Rechtsstaat*, I argue, leads to the alternatives of authoritarianism, on the one hand, or to an unattainable reversion to a simplified form of life, incompatible with advanced technology, on the other. If socialism is to be a reality, it must allow both popular access to the levers of power within a complex productive system and also the flourishing of Millian pluralism. To do this, it must have at its disposal a correspondingly complex constitutional system to guarantee the twin aspirations of democracy and pluralism and to mediate between them.

1

The 'New' Radicalism in Jurisprudence

An advanced legal system is complex and hierarchical. It embodies a system of rules which is both rigid, guaranteeing reliability and predictability, and flexible, allowing for successful application to particular cases and for development according to meta-rules of change. It is also characteristically reflexive and self-addressing, defining limits of constitutionally valid legal enactment. In striving for autonomy from executive power, it more or less successfully protects human rights with constitutional guarantees. As well as marking out limits within itself, it also endorses and sharpens a distinction of levels within society at large, in particular the distinction between the public and the private domains. In embodying forms of separation and differentiation, such a legal system has, in recent years, aroused the hostility of critics from both left and right.

The target of left wing critics has been its autonomization and hierarchization. Some ultra-left Marxists have envisaged the total destruction of the legal system, while more moderate critics have looked for its transformation, so as to become more immediate, accessible and 'responsive'.

Critics from the right have also stressed the advantages of immediacy and simplicity against what is taken to be the overweaning pretentions of constitutional rationality and have expressed antipathy to progressive legislation within the UK and to constitutional judgements imposed on the UK from without, by the EEC Court and by the European Court of Human Rights. Within the judiciary, an eminent spokesman has defended the traditions of English common law against these alien critical standards;[1] within academic jurisprudence, it has been argued that an advanced, legal society compares unfavourably with a simpler, customary society, in that the former has too much law and that it imposes standards on people from without, whereas the latter allows standards to develop naturally from within.[2]

The opposition between communitarianism and individualism as forms of organization was a central theme of nineteenth century social thought and we shall examine some of its intellectual history later in the book. The analytical models of *Gemeinschaft* and *Gesellschaft*, elaborated most fully by Ferdinand Tönnies, condensed and focused a century of work on the opposition and still provide a useful framework for our analysis of contemporary jurisprudence. At the heart of the *Gemeinschaft* for Tönnies is 'being together (*Zusammenwesen*), living together (*Zusammenwohen*) and working, or acting, together (*Zusammenwirken*)':[3] in it fellowship and immediacy are valued over the formality and rigidity of the abstract legal structure characteristic of the *Gesellschaft*.

Tönnies was adamant that his account of the *Gemeinschaft* model, for all its attractive features, was not to be taken as a plea for a 'return' to a vanished order or even for a passage to a new form of that order, since every society embodies a mixture of the two forms and there is no way of rolling back the tide of the *Gesellschaft*, as 'the essentially variable element which enhances culture but also transforms it into civilization'.[4] Critics of the modern legal order have been less circumspect than Tönnies in reaching explicit normative conclusions.[5]

1.1 THE LEFT CRITIQUE

On the left, the 'new' radical jurisprudence which emerged in the 1960s and 1970s on both sides of the Atlantic stemmed from Marxism, on the one hand, and from modern social theory, on the other, linked not only by a shared hostility to the established legal order, but also by a shared search for a new communitarian counter-order.

From Marxism

In jurisprudence, as elsewhere, the term 'Marxist' lacks clear denotation. In the recent literature it covers a range of diverse, indeed antagonistic, positions. The sober, ordered analytical work of Maureen Cain[6] and Alan Hunt,[7] drawing on the rational critical heritage of Marxism, is wholly at odds with the utopian millenarian rhetoric of Bankowski and Mungham.[8] Thus from within a Marxist standpoint Cain has characterized these latter authors as providing 'an overlay of marxist language on a foundation of libertarian humanism'.[9] Yet the mixture of 'materialist' critique and 'idealist' aspiration is inscribed within the Marxist classics themselves and the bizarre unreality of Bankowski's and Mungham's counter-model has its intellectual and political ancestry precisely within those classics. To disentangle the mixture, we need to return to the sources: not so much the anthologized citations of 'Marx and Engels on law' as to the texts which lie behind those citations. Within those texts, particularly in the *Grundrisse,* we shall uncover the ideological perspective of the withering-away of the law and the project of a new *Gemeinschaftlichkeit.* For the moment let us simply tabulate some of the features of the ultra-left picture of the present order (1) and the corresponding features of the envisaged order (2) present in explicit or implicit form in Bankowski's and Mungham's text.

First, (1) and (2) represent two rival models of the social system in general.[10] In (1),

(a) individualism reigns (the individual is 'king') (p. 31);
(b) power 'comes from the top' and is unequally distributed (p. 29);
(c) people are unfree and 'dehumanized', because 'denied the capacity to determine, self-consciously, their own lives' (p. 28);
(d) the social system is complex and 'highly fragile' (p. 30);
(e) administration is highly centralized and channelled through the State and the 'bureaucratic machine', composed of 'professionals' and 'experts' (p. 28);
(f) individuals' relations 'with each other and with the world' are 'obfuscated by various ideologies' (p. 31).

In (2), in contrast,

(a) 'man lives as a socialized being' without 'blockages to living communally';
(b) power 'comes from below', 'the people . . . have the power', 'proletarian power' is exercised;
(c) society is 'reorganized into one that is truly free';
(d) society is complex but free;
(e) 'mass democracy' operates through workers' councils, with part-time, 'instantly removable' delegates;
(f) individuals' relations 'with each other and with the world are obvious'.

Most of the component terms of these models will be examined in the course of the book, in particular the underlying contrast between individualism and communitarianism. It is characteristic of ultra-left writers to assert theses (c) and (f) together, envisaging that the denial of freedom and 'humanity' to individuals is determined in full or in part by their ideological 'obfuscation': a point of view which tends to reinforce, rather than reduce, the distance between 'the people' and the agents of their enlightenment.[11] The difficulty of dealing with 'complexity' from the ultra-left perspective emerges in the tabular presentation. For the authors were hostile to the 'complexity' of the present order, in so far as it demands professional managerial and administrative skills and in so far as the structure of an advanced, complex society is not immediately knowable by its individual members. Yet they wanted, at the same time, to allow for a 'complexity' of 'clashing diversities', without admitting the specialization of personnel apparently necessary for the orderly running of such a pluralist society.

Second, (1) and (2) represent two rival models of the legal order in particular. Here the authors' thoughts are more difficult to tabulate, since their picture of the legal order under (2) is so elusive.

In (1), Bankowski and Mungham saw the legal order as performing the functions of maintaining the property rights of those in control and of neutralizing the power of the proletariat: these functions being exercised both by 'overt repression' and by the 'ideological' legitimation of authority (p. 28).

They deemed this legitimation process to be 'ideological' in the sense that it was a sham. To substantiate this general thesis, they chose illustrative examples which were, to say the least, tendentious, including Rhodesia under the illegal Smith regime and the North of Ireland.

Of Rhodesia, Bankowski and Mungham wrote, in 1976, that 'Ian Smith has concerned himself with legitimacy, even though his party is in complete and effective control of the country' (p. 12). By this they meant that the Smith regime sought formal recognition by the Rhodesian High Court, rather than recognition of the regime by the mass of the people as the legitimate source of authority. What characterized the regime was, indeed, the combination of coercion on the one hand and sham legitimation on the other: hence the appearance of 'complete and effective control' turned out to be short-lived. What was missing was the phenomenon for which the ultra-left critics had no place: legitimation, in the sense of popular endorsement through formally constituted judicial organs.

The authors' reference to inquiries into the legality or illegality of the British army's interrogation methods in the North of Ireland took the same form. They commented:

> Little space was devoted to questioning the morality of what were virtually disorientation techniques. If it could be shown that it was legal, then it was beyond question. In this way political questions are not only deflected but are made to seem entirely inappropriate. As long as the given social order is said to be legal then the world is all right. It is good because it is 'legal' and 'legal' stands outside the social structure and so guarantees it. (p. 13)

But only an *a priori* commitment to the thesis that the law is a sham would have blinded the authors to the role of the European Commission and Court of Human Rights in 'controlling the discretion of States' and thus raising 'the standards of human rights from the levels based on the history and complacency of the nineteenth and early twentieth centuries',[12] in particular to the Court's judgement that the United Kingdom's treatment of detainees had infringed Article 3 of the Convention, prohibiting torture or inhuman or degrading treatment or punishment.[13] The fact that the British government changed its practices following this judgement and that it and the governments of other signatory states did the same after other adverse judgements[14] suggests that neither component of the ultra-left critique is necessarily correct. First, it is not true that higher legal organs must conflate morality and positive law: the European Commission and Court embody the attempt, which has been not wholly vain, to make concrete human (moral) rights in a form which allows for their critical application to positive (municipal) law.[15] Second, it is not true that the law must be the mere passive register of political power. The range of the autonomy of the law is neither set down for all time in virtue of the law's unchanging nature nor is it a mere chimera. Rather it is determined by the particular balance of power domestically between citizens and executive, internationally between government and government.[16]

Bankowski and Mungham identified another dimension of the law's ideological function within the courtroom itself. Drawing on Heller's *Catch 22*, they characterized all formalized rule-governed interrogation procedure as a 'degradation ceremony' (p. 93); alternatively, by comparing legal process with professional wrestling (as interpreted by Roland Barthes) they found it to be a con trick (p. 97).

But, against this critical model of the given legal order, their counter-model was elusive. In general, their aim was to debunk the majesty of the law, envisaging that it would play only a marginal role in the organization of the envisaged order, where individualism, capitalism and repression would supposedly be absent (p. 31). Since there will, allegedly, be no need for policing and no 'complex regulations' to be enforced (p. 30) and since its ideological role will be redundant in the new realm of transparency, law, we are told, 'will genuinely wither away' (p. 30), even though 'in "socialist diversity", legality will in some sense reappear because it will help to ease the problems of clashing diversities' (pp. 30–1). Whether the authors intended any serious theoretical distinction between the terms 'law' and '"legality"' (their quotation marks) cannot be determined from a reading of their text. In the absence of such a distinction, the apparently direct contradiction between the two passages cited does no more than mark the locus of a problem deep within the Marxist tradition.

At the same time, they wanted to show that the law was irrelevant as an instrument for changing the present order: 'the law will not change capitalist society' (p. 28); and in a set of oppositions they contrasted the legalistic approach to transformation (1) with their own libertarian approach (2):

(1)	(2)
the taking out of injunctions	the taking over of unoccupied houses
the implementation of further nationalization and participation measures	the taking over of factories and entire industries
making illegal the 'unacceptable face of capitalism'	the taking over of the entire society (p. 29)

In each case, we find structures, relations and rules devalued relative to direct 'actions': there is no allusion to the insight of Wittgenstein, Hart and, arguably, Marx that all practice is mediated through rule-governed structures of relatively enduring social relations. Bankowski and Mungham were but reviving a recurring theme in ultra-left Marxism from the early Lukács of *History and Class Consciousness*[17] to the Sartre of *Critique of Dialectical Reason*[18] when they reduced the universal relation structure/practice to the particular relation oppressive structure/ideologically mystified practice. From such a perspective, it is unsurprising to find almost no residual role for law, that most highly articulated system of rule-governed behaviour, in the new envisaged social order. Hostility to rule structures, expressed in the pejorative use of the terms 'performance', 'game', 'ritual', 'theatre', etc. is allied to the myth of transparency, the vision of a society in which something 'standing behind' the set of available social roles and relations (human subjectivity, perhaps) will be revealed in a social order which will have become 'obvious' to the participants. Never wholly absent from either Rousseau[19] or Marx[20] and explicitly present in Sartre's *Being and Nothing-*

ness, the myth of transparency reappears in each new variant of utopian social critique.

From modern social theory

R. M. Unger was inspired more directly by Max Weber than by Marx and attempted to incorporate a reading of traditional natural law theory into his subtle, intricate and elusive critique of modern society, which could not be more different from Bankowski's and Mungham's brash philistinism. Where they eschewed reflection on the intellectual history of their position, Unger's project was precisely 'to help one understand the context of ideas and sentiments within which philosophy and politics must now be practised'.[21] At the same time, there is an element of continuity between Unger's work and that of the other left critics of the contemporary legal order in his vision of 'a kind of thought and society that does not yet and may never exist'. It is to this vision that we shall briefly turn our attention, ignoring the richness of Unger's historical and methodological analysis. Unger offered no crude counter-position of model and conter-model, but rather an account of what he saw as the immanent, inescapable contradictions of 'modernity' and the lineaments of an envisaged 'solution' contained therein.

P. Nonet and P. Selznick were to operate with a similar typology to Unger's and to reach normative conclusions not far from his, though more closely related to recent political and legal developments in the USA. We shall glance at their account at the conclusion of the chapter.

For Unger, western legal history has passed through three stages:[22] (1) 'bureaucratic law with its public and positive rules', used as a direct instrument of central political power (p. 238); (2) 'the rule of law, with its commitment to the generality and the autonomy of legal norms' and to 'the distinction among legislation, administration and adjudication' (p. 191); (3) 'post-liberal society', the era of 'the welfare trend' in law, which 'moves the rule of law ideal back in the direction of bureaucratic law by undermining the social and ideological bases of that ideal' (p. 238). In it, 'the State's pretense to being a neutral guardian of the social order' is abandoned (p. 193).

Unger's romantic pessimism, noted by Talcott Parsons,[23] is notable in his analysis both of legal autonomy and formalism, dominant at stage 2, and of the unstable mixture of the remnants of the rule of law with purposive legislation and adjudication in welfare capitalism (stage 3).

For Unger, the inherent defect of formalism is that it is incompatible with two other fundamental social values: equity and solidarity. Unger saw it as incompatible with equity in so far as it could not be used to address substantive questions of justice, morality and economic and political power: this had been the guiding theme of the Marxist critique of legal abstraction. But why must formalism, in which 'the mere invocation of rules and the deduction of conclusions from them is believed sufficient for every authoritative legal choice' (p. 194) conflict with those other values? Unger gave a curious answer: 'equal treatment of unequal situations by the judiciary simply confirms, if it does not aggravate, their inequality.' (p. 191) Now this looks like a serious mistake, one which was clearly identified by H. L. A. Hart in 1961:[24]

> There is a certain complexity in the structure of the idea of justice. . . . it consists of two parts: a uniform or constant feature, summarized in the precept 'Treat like cases alike' and a shifting or varying criterion used in determining when, for any given purpose, cases are alike or different.
>
> . . . it is plain that the law itself cannot now determine what resemblances and differences among individuals the law must recognize if its rules are to treat like cases alike and so be just. Here accordingly there is much room for doubt and dispute. Fundamental differences, in general moral and political outlook, may lead to irreconcilable differences and disagreement as to what characteristics of human beings are to be taken as relevant for the criticism of law as unjust.

This elementary, but essential, insight of Hart must cast doubt on Unger's pessimistic thesis that there is a necessary connection between (1) a commitment to formalism, as defined above, which is equivalent to Hart's principle of abstract procedural justice, and (2) a commitment to conservatism concerning the given political order, in particular to the given distribution of power. There is no such necessary connection for precisely the reason Hart suggested: namely that a legal formalist, who may believe in the strict application of the rules of procedural justice, according to the book, may also be a political radical, whose aim is the drastic rewriting of the criteria of similarity and difference: as a proponent of reverse discrimination, for instance, he would consistently assert social deprivation in virtue of race as a relevant criterion of difference, demanding systematic (formalistic) treatment in legislation and adjudication.[25]

For Unger formalism conflicts with solidarity in asserting that legal entitlements must be absolute, that they cannot be tempered or limited by broader social goals:[26]

> A legal order confers entitlements and obligations; the more formal it becomes, the more does it treat each entitlement as a power to be exercised in the direction of the powerholder. (p. 207)

Yet this thesis can be understood only as expressing the lineaments of the abstract model of the *Gesellschaft*, rather than its exemplification in concrete legal systems. As Lloyd has pointed out concerning the alleged absoluteness of the right of ownership in contemporary law, the idea that the owner may 'do anything he likes' with his property[27]

> . . . fails for two obvious reasons, namely, because ownership may be virtually completely divested of the elements of enjoyment and control and still remain ownership, and, further, because there is no such thing in law as an unlimited right, for the law will inevitably impose restraints on the use or disposal of property. In earlier systems the main restraint may have been fetters imposed by the criminal law, but in modern times the huge development of the public-law aspect of property has confined within very narrow limits the potential freedoms of the property–owner.

In order to demonstrate that no satisfactory compromise can be found between formalism, expressed in private property rights, and solidarity, expressed in a set of socially desirable limitations on those rights, the opposition needs to be anchored in a solider historico-sociological context than Unger provided.

At the heart of Unger's criticism of formalism is the thought that it must foster 'systematic disparities of power' or, at least, leave unsolved 'the basic problem of unjustified power' (p. 211). But that thought gains plausibility only when legality is linked more or less definitionally to political conservatism. When that link is broken, when the two components of Hart's formula for procedural justice are distinguished, there is no inherent reason for thinking that legality, understood as the commitment to formalized rule-governed procedures, should conflict with other social values.

The conflict between legality and equity takes the form, for Unger, of a conflict between formalism, abstraction and universalism, on the one hand, and responsiveness to the particular case, on the other. Equity is seen as 'the polar opposite to justification by rules . . . the intuitive sense of justice in the particular case.' (p. 205) A similar conflict was claimed between legality, operating 'through rules established before disputes arise' and solidarity's 'procedures of justification that resist clear-cut rules' (p. 206), relying on the 'moral sense of the community', which 'seems to transcend any system of rules or principles in which one tries to express or encase it'. But, if equity-solidarity is to mark an irreducible polar opposite to legality, it must be shown that it arises from an irreducible opposition between pre-established rules, on the one hand, and the 'moral sense of the community', on the other. But, stated baldly, that idea too is implausible. For rules which in no way preceded the disputes to which they were to be applied would cease to be rules at all. Even the most informal procedures for dispute settlement must be recognizable as such prior to the presentation of particular disputes, even though no written code might encompass them: otherwise the distinction between rule and case must disappear.

Thus the alleged polarity between legality-formalism and equity-solidarity loses its sharpness, appears to be more a matter of degree, in the light of Hart's distinction between procedural justice, on the one hand, and criteria of relevant similarity and difference, on the other, and in the light also of the evident non-polarity of the universalism/particularity distinction in the application of rules. There appears to be no *a priori* obstacle to our reaching a working consensus at any one time concerning the shifting and developing Hartian criteria in legislation and concerning the play between formality and responsiveness in adjudication.

Unger's pessimism extended beyond his analysis of these abstract models for comprehending the development of the law to the concrete analysis of the present order and the prospects for transforming it. The present order of welfare liberalism for Unger marks 'the disintegration of the rule of law' (p. 192), in particular the 'undermining' of 'the relative generality and the autonomy that distinguishes the legal order from other kinds of law' (p. 197).

The contemporary lawyer, for Unger, is faced by:

> A style of legal discourse that eats away at generality and autonomy without necessarily increasing one's assurance that he is doing justice. The attempted compromise between formalism and equity is inherently dissatisfying and unstable; it does not resolve the problem of subjective value that lies at the root of the dilemma of formality and equity, nor need it contribute to transform the circumstances of domination that deprive people of confidence in their own moral judgments. (pp. 209–10)

Unger's pessimism is marked by the modal words: '*inherently* dissatisfying and unstable', 'without *necessarily* increasing one's assurance' and 'nor *need* it contribute' [my italics]. The question which poses itself is this, The present legal order is, of course, unstable, in just the sense that Unger suggested, but in what sense is that unstable order 'dissatisfying' and that dissatisfaction 'inherent'? Unger had in mind the experience of dissatisfaction when inconsistent 'ideals' or models of jurisprudence were put into practice, expressed in

> . . . a greater willingness to regard as part of the law certain moral conceptions that do not seem capable of development and application in ways consistent with the ideals of generality and autonomy. For these conceptions can neither be reduced to rules nor divorced from views about moral obligation. (p. 210)

But, using the Hartian distinction between form and criteria, we must question whether there is a necessary incompatibility between welfare law on the one hand and 'the ideals of generality and autonomy' on the other. For Unger the exhaustive alternatives for the relation between law and morality are identity (reducibility) or polar opposition (divorce). But this is a curious position. *Prima facie*, there seems to be a third possibility, namely that, with a degree of moral consensus, an advanced pluralist society can endorse *both* (1) purposive legislation concerning social goals, the allocation of resources, redistribution of wealth, etc. *and* (2) a system of personal civil rights which precludes the overriding of specific, itemized rights for instrumental purposive goals and defends the expression of a plurality of values in a plurality of forms of life against public and private interference. That the combination of (1) and (2) makes for instability is, from a less pessimistic standpoint, a virtue rather than a vice of the present order.

It is interesting to find that Unger did, in fact, reach a conclusion very much like the above by the end of his book, after distinguishing the dangers inscribed in both welfare liberalism, the unstable equilibrium between formalism and instrumentalism, and its main rival, 'revolutionary socialist society' (pp. 231 ff.), where formalism is almost wholly sacrificed to instrumentalism and individual interests to collective bonds and social roles.

Carefully avoiding the problems inscribed in the historicist vocabulary of Hegel and Marx (negation of the negation, recall, etc.), Unger favoured

> . . . the metaphor of a spiral that reverses direction without returning to its starting point. This would mean that individual freedom could be rescued from the demise of the rule of law and brought into harmony with the reassertion of communitarian concerns. It would also signify that the capacity to see and to treat each form of social life as a creation rather than as a fate could survive the disintegration of public and positive law and be reconciled with the sense of an immanent order in society. (p. 239)

He then proceeded to sketch *de novo* the lineaments of democratic pluralism, as though, for this reader and absorber of virtually the whole history of European social thought, J. S. Mill's *On Liberty* had never been written! The virtue of liberalism, for Unger, had been 'its efficacy in preventing immediate government oppression of the individual'; its vices that (1) it had left 'basic relations of work and everyday life' at the mercy of illegitimate, uncontrolled power, and (2) it had endangered ties of solidarity, group loyalty and community. The latter could, on Unger's view be salvaged, without sacrificing individual freedom or licensing a return to 'tribalism' (p. 238) by moving, not back to custom, but up the spiral to 'customary law' (p. 241), which marks the final point of Unger's vision. The envisaged order is based on a degree of consensus that pluralism is to be valued in itself:

> Openness toward the future means that one must value the conflictual process by which communities are created over time and satisfactory relations are established among them as much as the internal cohesion of any communal group. (p. 241)

Moreover

> This customary law would have many of the marks we associate with custom: its lack of a positive and a public character and its largely emergent and implicity quality. Yet it would differ from custom in making room for a distinction between what is and what ought to be. It would become less the stable normative order of a particular group than the developing moral language of mankind. (p. 241)

The position I shall defend in the course of the book converges closely with Unger's. Like him, I shall argue that personal and cultural pluralism is possible in advanced societies and that it is compatible with interventionist legislation capable of altering the balance of power between social classes and between citizens and state. Like him, I shall emphasize the qualitative differences between the forms of life of traditional (integrated *Gemeinschaft*) societies and pluralist (*gesellschaftlich*) societies. Like him, I shall argue that a relatively freely chosen *Gemeinschaft* within a modern pluralist society is, in turn, qualitatively different from a traditional *Gemeinschaft* which is inherited, imposed and relatively closed: a distinction between a form of life 'seen as a creation rather than a fate'.

I envisage a social order in which the overarching framework is rights-based and constitutional, but within which a plurality of *Gemeinschaften*, based on a plurality of principles, can flourish, their existence legally defended. In my picture, this tension between the principles dominant at the macro and the micro levels is irreducible, but not necessarily destructive. Unger, in one great tradition of natural law, sought, but could not find, a greater level of homogeneity between levels than is envisaged by me. For me, then, the problems of interaction between the relatively closed *Gemeinschaften*, with their own sets of rules, and the overarching constitutional *Gesellschaft*, is central, not marginal.

I am suspicious, like Unger, of the mythology of return to a simple, immediate, closed *Gemeinschaft*. But I am, perhaps, more historicist than he in thinking that such a return is impossible because of the material facts of modern technology, in particular information technology: unless we have a formalized, enforceable system of rights, then, assuming that we have not reverted to the immediacy of primitive, low technology social relations, we cannot prevent the illegitimate monopolization of power by particular groups.

I conclude this brief survey of left critiques of the present legal order with a comment on Nonet's and Selznick's *Law and Society in Transition*, a book which owes much to Unger's typology of legal orders.[28] Unger had distinguished bureaucratic, formalistic and welfare-liberal forms and had remained pessimistic about the possibility of successfully resolving the tensions inscribed within the latter without moving towards a qualitatively new form, customary law. He had also eschewed any concrete account of the possible mechanism of this envisaged transition: hence the somewhat utopian flavour of his final model-building. Nonet and Selznick, in contrast, anchored their analysis more firmly in contemporary developments in the law in the United States.

Nonet and Selznick distinguished three modalities or basic states of law-in-society: (1) law as the servant of repressive power, (2) law as a differentiated institution capable of taming repression and protecting its own integrity and (3) law as a facilitator of response to social needs and aspirations (pp. 14–15).[29] These three types (repressive law, autonomous law and responsive law) were presented as the characteristic forms of law of different types of political order, as 'different modalities of legal experience', reflected in different forms of jurisprudence, e.g. command theories, positivism and legal realism (pp. 17–18), and as 'stages of evolution in the relation of law to the political and social order' (p. 18). The second stage, autonomous law, theorized in the jurisprudence of Hart, has four characteristics, according to Nonet and Selznick: (1) it proclaims the independence of the judiciary, the separation of law from politics; (2) its legal order espouses the 'model of rules'; (3) procedural fairness and regularity is promoted over substantive justice; (4) 'fidelity to law' is understood as strict obedience to the rules of positive law. Criticism of existing laws must be channelled through the political process (p. 54). Nonet's and Selznick's account of the separation of powers, allowing both for restraint on arbitrary political power and for a process of double legitimation, of the political power by the law and of the law by itself, was masterly and subtle. So too was their account of the '*potential* for legal development' within autonomous law itself, stemming from the tension between 'its capacity to restrain the authority of rulers and limit the obligations of citizens' and the 'unanticipated result' thereof, namely that it 'encourages a posture of criticism that contributes to the erosion of the rule of law', in short to 'a rights-centered jurisprudence' (p. 71). In their developmental model, they proceeded to map the development of the new form of 'responsive law', in particular the rise of 'social advocacy' in the United States, in which

> . . . legal action comes to serve as a vehicle by which groups and organizations may participate in the determination of public policy. It is less exclusively perceived as a way of vindicating individual claims based on recognized rules. (p. 96)

This transition was recognized by the Supreme Court in its 1963 judgement in favour of the NAACP (National Association for the Advancement of Colored People). Now Nonet and Selznick were clearly correct in identifying this new stage in the confident assertion of constitutional rights by individuals and groups in the United States. Indeed one would assume from their analysis that this stage marked a strengthening of the rule of law in so far as

Social advocacy invokes legal authority and uses forums that can be held accountable to legal rules and principles. Hence, the characteristic locale of such advocacy is the court or the administrative agency rather than legislative bodies. The appeal is to legal entitlement, not to political will. (p. 97)

It is of course true that recognition of 'group rights', in particular in counter-discrimination legislation, does conflict with the legal individualism characteristic of autonomous law.[30] In this sense there has been an important shift from the civil rights struggles of the 1960s, a passage from 'formally ignoring' to 'formally recognizing' the facts of 'multi-ethnic diversity' in the United States and elsewhere.[31] It is also true that this passage has put to the test (as every major political development does) the relative public consensus concerning the criteria of justice and fair play.

But Nonet and Selznick wanted to identify a more fundamental, more 'dialectical' feature of the transition, such that responsive law would emerge as a kind of synthesis of the two previous forms. In this synthesis, the new pluralism would bring about the dilution of sovereignty into a 'loose aggregate of public corporations', which would constitute nothing less than 'the withering away of the state' (p. 102). In it the distinction between the legal and the political would not be annihilated (as in repressive law), but rather

. . . government acts in a dual capacity. As a *political* actor it assumes responsibility for deciding what ends are to be pursued and what resources it is prepared to commit in dealing with problems such as pollution control or discrimination in employment . . . as a *legal* actor, [it] establish[es] the agencies and mechanisms by which public ends will be furthered. (p. 112)

While the allusion to the 'withering away of the state' might be taken as a piece of harmless rhetoric in the American context, the vocabulary of the 'dual capacity' of government, of the replacement of adjudication by 'regulation' (p. 108),[32] must be viewed with some scepticism in that it suggests a process in which the independence of the judiciary is down-graded, the idea of citizens having rights against the state loses its force and indeed questions concerning rights are replaced by questions concerning administrative convenience. This process, already well advanced in certain societies, is not easily reversed, nor is there reason to think that 'values and interests . . . given short shrift in the politics of majority rule' (p. 96) would be better protected in Nonet's and Selznick's system of devolved sovereignty without a formal, institutionalized division of powers than it is in the more integrated societies we presently inhabit.

1.2 THE RIGHT CRITIQUE

The common law vs. the abstract Rechtsstaat

Lord Denning, self-appointed champion of 'the freedom of the individual as against the state and the bureaucrats',[33] has also been, to the surprise of some observers,[34] an opponent of either the enactment of a new Bill of Rights in this country or of the entrenchment of the European Convention of Human Rights in its constitution. His opposition has been based in part on a gut reaction characteristic of quite primitive right-wing politicians, namely a fear of 'disgruntled people who will bring proceedings before the courts challenging the orderly system of our country'.[35]

In the case of the European Convention, we cannot ignore in the right's reaction a degree of xenophobia, characterized by Patricia Hewitt as distrust of '"interference" of foreign institutions with decisions of the British Parliament or British courts'.[36] The reaction is in keeping with a tradition going back to Burke[37] of hostility to abstract, formally embodied constitutional principles and, corresponding to that hostility, a positive adherence to more informal norms of fair play, interpreted by judges with considerable powers of discretion:[38]

'What is important, above all, is a country's political climate and traditions.' In England the importance is enshrined in the independence of the judges. They have managed very well in the past to form and maintain human rights and fundamental freedoms. They created most of them by their decisions. You can trust them to continue to do so.

For Lord Denning, the citizen's liberties are founded on 'the independence of the judges', but not on a set of general principles to which he can appeal in the active pursuit of his constitutional rights: a form of benign paternalism which prevents[39]

People praying in aid of . . . [their] fundamental rights, as they say, and giving much embarrassment and disturbance to society.

In Burke's more eloquent words:[40]

. . . the restraints on men, as well as their liberties, are to be reckoned among their rights. But as the liberties and the restrictions vary with times and circumstances, and admit of infinite modifications, they cannot be settled upon any abstract rule; and nothing is so foolish as to discuss them upon that principle.

For Lord Denning and other critics from the right, the European Convention embodies just that kind of 'abstract rule', imposing constraints on the British judiciary which would impede its particular idiosyncratic brand of 'independence'. Defenders of civil liberties, however, have every reason to question Lord Denning's complacency. In Britain there is only an informal division of powers between executive and judiciary, the appointment of judges 'lies wholly in the hands of politicians',[41] there is no written constitution or contemporary Bill of Rights and there is little legal protection of citizens' privacy or legal control of the endemic secrecy of government and civil service. In his concluding judgement on the European institutions Ralph Beddard held that:[42]

Recent decisions . . . seem to show that the Commission and Court finally realise that their function in controlling the discretion of States is pre-eminent, and that it is the chief way in which they are able to raise the standards of human rights from the levels based on the history and complacency of the nineteenth and early twentieth centuries.

The hostile reaction to these institutions from the right in this country suggests that Beddard's judgement was correct.

The conflict between civil libertarians, attempting to enforce supra-national norms, and Denning, entrenching English law against alien interference, echoes that of nearly two centuries ago, as Burke reacted to the European, particularly French, Enlightenment ideology of constitutionalism, 'the idea that rationally articulated, clear and comprehensive codes would be the instruments of social advance'.[43] The great bearer of that ideology in this country was Jeremy Bentham, who expressed his Enlightenment confidence in codifications and commentaries of immense detail. He connected 'the English form of government – a mixture, composed of monarchico-aristocratical despotism with a spice of anarchy'[44] with its lack of a rational legal system. Hegel reached the same conclusion in his late pamphlet 'The English Reform Bill':[45]

Hitherto England has lacked the features which constitute the major part of these glorious and fortunate advances [of the Enlightenment]. Amongst these features the chief is the scientific remodelling of law, whereby, on the one hand, general principles have been applied to and carried through the particular specifications [of law] and their complexities, while on the other hand concrete and special cases have been reduced to simpler provisions.

For him it was self-evident that:[46]

The reason why England is so remarkably far behind the other civilized states of Europe in institutions derived from true rights is simply that there the governing power lies in the hands of those possessed of so many privileges which contradict a rational constitutional law and true legislation.

It would be wrong to underestimate the resilience of the British tradition of haphazard, piecemeal constitutional freedoms, 'concessions wrung by force, or else acts of grace, agreements, etc., and constitutional rights . . . struck by the form of private rights'.[47] Key components of the *Rechtsstaat*, the rights to trial by jury, assumption of innocence, *habeas corpus,* etc., so eloquently defended by E. P. Thompson as part of the particularly British legal-political heritage, are indeed the prize won by that piecemeal struggle. But they are also now under constant threat. As citizens' civil liberties become increasingly vulnerable from the agents of an increasingly powerful state, it is clear that the common law provides them with only the most fragile protection, particularly at moments perceived by their rulers to be times of emergency.[48] The opposition between Burke and Bentham is now more urgent than ever.[49]

Anthropological romanticism

The work of anthropologists like Gluckman, Moore and Allott[50] has opened the world of 'pre-modern' law to the non-specialist. Apart from its intrinsic fascination, their work is valuable in dispelling a number of prejudices widely held by the general public and by speculators within jurisprudence concerning 'primitive' law. Simplistic evolutionary schemata, founded on hazy conceptions of the repressive, arbitrary, discontinuous nature of imaginary primitive systems compared with developed ones have to be modified or abandoned in the face of information concerning their real subtlety, flexibility and sophistication.[51] At the same time, anthropologists are, by the nature of their discipline, tempted by a certain nostalgia for simpler forms,[52] approximately more closely to the *Gemeinschaft,* particularly when they allow themselves to indulge in explicit normative recommendations concerning the shortcomings of the present order in our own advanced societies.

Antony Allott's *The Limits of Law* is an example of just this combination of the analytic and the normative. He gives a masterly account of the disastrous effect of 'translocating' West European legal codes to colonies whose economy and kinship structures did not correspond to those of the metropolis where laws had been developed to regulate capitalist corporations and monogamous atomic families. He contrasts customary law, where there is a degree of consensus concerning legitimacy and familiarity with the law's content, with the alien, unaccepted, ignored quality of the imposed western codes. His description of the ineffective process of 'translocation', whether practised by the European colonial rulers or by their Europeanized successors, is convincing in its detail. His normative conclusion for advanced societies is less so. Using an implicit analogy from imperialist 'translocation', Allott seeks to question the use of 'law as programme', within our own societies, 'where the legislator, eager to reconstruct society to his image, is no longer willing to wait, to leave transformation to occur as the piecemeal and eventual result of countless individual decisions' (p. 174).[53] For Allott, the use of 'law as programme' is the work of individuals who are 'arrogant' and 'impatient' (p. 175). Their Enlightenment illusion, for him, is the idea that social problems can be solved by legislation, from above, in the absence of 'education and persuasion' (p. 236) from below. Allott is of course correct in seeing that no legislation can be effective in a vacuum, deprived of popular legitimating endorsement. But his 'translocation' analogy obscures the complex phenomenon of legitimation in an advanced society operating with some tradition of both constitutionality and democratic government. From the premiss that in India 'Legislation against discrimination on caste grounds seems to have had minimal effect on social practices or attitudes.' (p. 236) he concludes that in Britain legislation against sexual and racial discrimination is likely to be equally ineffective: '. . . the elaborate structure of anti-discrimination legislation is misconceived and self-defeating.' (p. 236).

The force of the analogy should be considered a little more closely. The two cases are held to be similar in that both pieces of legislation encounter popular resistance from 'a group or class with something to lose'. That group may face losing a position of economic or political privilege or may be forced to 'dismantle their own psychology as well as their domestic role' (p. 201). But now the limits of the analogy can be discerned. First, at the ideological level (what Allott calls 'their own psychology'), there is every difference between the belief-systems sustaining the two cultures. If we contrast the ideological obstacles facing on the one hand anti-caste legislation in

India and on the other hand sex-equality legislation in Britain, we find that they are of a different order. In the one system, belief in the given inequality is a component of a total religious cultural world view; in the other, it is an anomaly, increasingly deprived of intellectual credentials. Second, there is a history of successful struggle for sexual equality in the developed countries, marked by legislation allowing women to be property-owners, voters, students, etc. with the same rights as men. In so far as this struggle has entered a new phase, seeking positive discrimination legislation to make equal rights in employment a reality, it is not radically out of step with the democratic-egalitarian tendency of our social development. Third, the claim that in our societies particular pieces of 'radical' legislation are imposed on a recalcitrant citizenry by an elite of legislators alienated from the popular will also needs examination. The theory of constitutional government is that there is interaction between legislation and popular opinion. Even where that interaction is imperfect, it is possible that detailed legislation may precede popular opinion up to a point, though it cannot survive a systematic and sustained divorce from it. At the same time, a commitment to constitutional principles may call for fair treatment for particular groups in society, even in the face of resistance by individuals and groups adversely affected thereby. How far a particular *Rechtsstaat* can mediate between these two poles (popular endorsement vs. constitutional protection of the unpopular) depends on its level of political culture and sophistication.[54] But in a society where constitutional values are relatively firmly entrenched, where citizens have some real access both to the making and to the application of the law,[55] there is reason to think that programmatic law-making need not be perceived wholly as an alien imposition. It may approximate more to Rawls' conception of civil disobedience, in which[56]

> . . . one addresses the sense of justice of the majority of the community and declares that in one's considered opinion the principles of social cooperation among free and equal men are not being respected.

Of course the parallel is approximate. Programmatic legislation is not just an appeal to the majority's 'sense of justice'. Allott's objection is that it goes beyond an appeal in invoking the coercive force of law. But in a social order where legitimacy is derived from some degree of popular endorsement and of respect for constitutional rights and where direct coercion is relatively rare, I would argue that programmatic legislation can properly be understood as an attempt to make concrete principles of fairness generally accepted at the abstract level of the constitution, but in practice flouted by particular economic, educational, or cultural rules or practices. Allott alleges, it will be recalled, that there is a parallel between anti-caste legislation, on the one hand, and anti-discrimination legislation here and in the United States, on the other. That parallel holds only if the 'sense of justice of the majority of the community' in our countries excludes consideration of women and racial minorities as full and equal members of the *Rechtsstaat*. Such pessimism, I would submit, is unfounded.

NOTES

1. Lord Denning, *What Next in the Law,* 1982.
2. A. Allott, *The Limits of Law,* 1980.
3. F. Tönnies, *On Sociology, Pure, Applied and Empirical,* 1971, p. 69.
4. Ibid., pp. 9–10.
5. Tönnies's work will be examined in section 4.1.
6. M. Cain, 'The main themes of Marx's and Engels' sociology of law', 1974.
7. A. Hunt, 'The politics of law and justice', 1981.
8. Z. Bankowski and G. Mungham, *Images of Law,* 1976.
9. M. Cain, Review of Bankowski and Mungham, *Images of Law.*
10. Page references in this section of the text are to Z. Bankowski and G. Mungham, *Images of Law.*
11. As noted by Maureen Cain in her review.
12. R. Beddard, *Human Rights and Europe,* 1980, pp. 173–4.
13. Ibid., p. 101. The case was brought by Ireland against the United Kingdom (*Ireland* v. *United Kingdom,* 5310/71 Eur. Court H. R. Series A, No. 25).
14. See R. Beddard, *Human Rights and Europe,* p. 175.

15. This is the underlying theme of R. Dworkin's account of the US Constitution in *Taking Rights Seriously*.
16. Domestic: see E. P. Thompson, 'The State versus its "enemies"' in *Writing by Candlelight*, 1980. International: R. Beddard, *Human Rights and Europe*, chapters 8, 9 and 10.
17. For Lukács's own perceptive self-criticism, written in 1967, see *History and Class Consciousness*, p. xxiv.
18. J-P. Sartre, *Critique of Dialectical Reason*, 1976, p. 417.
19. For an extended, brilliant exposition of this theme in Rousseau, see J. Starobinski, *Jean-Jacques Rousseau: la transparence et l'obstacle*. In his account of *La Nouvelle Héloise* in chapter 5, he identified the contrast between *théâtre*, where there are intermediaries, obstacles, and *fête*, where there are none and where the distance between actor and spectator is negated in 'pure freedom, pure transparency, continuous with other freedoms, other transparencies' (p. 121).
20. See chapter 3.
21. R. M. Unger, *Knowledge and Politics*, 1975, p. v.
22. R. M. Unger, *Law in Modern Society*, 1976. All page references in the text of this section are to that book.
23. T. Parsons, Review of *Law in Modern Society*, p. 148.
24. H. L. A. Hart, *The Concept of Law*, 1961, pp. 156–7.
25. Cf. R. Dworkin, 'Reverse Discrimination' in *Taking Rights Seriously*, 1977.
26. This emerges in Tönnies's table of oppositions between *Gemeinschaft* and *Gesellschaft*.
27. D. Lloyd, *The Idea of Law*, 1973, pp. 321–2. Lloyd illustrated the point:

    > To give but one instance, the extent to which a landowner is limited as regards his mode of use, control, and present or future disposition of the land, by a heavy overlay of town-planning and building regulations and possible powers of compulsory acquisition of the land by various authorities, sufficiently emphasizes that ownership is not so much a general liberty of a man to do what he likes with his own, but is much more in the nature of some kind of residual right which remains after all other relevant rights and restraints have been duly discounted.

    Limitations to absolute ownership come too from the Highways Act 1959, Section 134, enjoining the owners of property 'to keep hedges, trees, or shrubs trimmed so as not to impede the passage of pedestrians or vehicles', as the author was informed by a recent communication from the local City Engineer's Department! For further discussion, see A. M. Honoré, 'Ownership', 1961, especially section V.

28. As acknowledged in P. Nonet and P. Selznick, *Law and Society in Transition*, 1978, pp. 53–4.
29. Page references in the text of this section are to Nonet and Selznick, *Law and Society in Transition*.
30. See especially N. Glazer, 'Individual rights against group rights', 1978.
31. N. Glazer, 'Individual rights against group rights', p. 98 See also R. Dworkin, 'Reverse discrimination' in *Taking Rights Seriously*.
32. I shall return to this topic in the discussion of Pashukanis and Kamenka and Tay in sections 4.2 and 4.3 below.
33. Quoted by E. Young, 'Developing a system of administrative law?', 1981, p. 171.
34. See M. Zander, *A Bill of Rights?*, 1979, p. 68.
35. Quoted by M. Zander, ibid.
36. P. Hewitt, *The Abuse of Power*, 1982, p. 231.
37. E. Burke, *Reflections on the Revolution in France*, 1969 edition.
38. Lord Denning, *What Next in the Law*, p. 303.
39. Quoted by M. Zander, *A Bill of Rights?*, p. 68.
40. E. Burke, *Reflections on the Revolution in France*, p. 151.
41. J. A. G. Griffith, *The Politics of the Judiciary*, 1981, p. 151.
42. R. Beddard, *Human Rights and Europe*, pp. 173–4.
43. H. L. A. Hart, Introduction to J. Bentham, *Introduction to the Principles of Morals and Legislation*, p. xxxvi.
44. J. Bentham, *Constitutional Code*, 1983 edition, p. 25.
45. G. W. F. Hegel, *PW*, p. 300.
46. Ibid.
47. Ibid., p. 299. For Engels's endorsement of this tradition see section 3.3 below.
48. This has been argued most clearly and forcefully by Lord Scarman, the outstanding spokesman of the British judiciary for the entrenchment of civil rights. See P. Hewitt, *The Abuse of Power*, p. 243.
49. For a detailed critical discussion of Lord Denning's jurisprudence, see E. Young, 'Developing a system of administrative law?'. On Burke and Hegel, see J-F. Suter, 'Burke, Hegel and the French Revolution', 1971.
50. Particularly useful is Max Gluckman's collection *The Allocation of Responsibility* and S. F. Moore's essay in that collection, 'Legal liability and evolutionary interpretation'.
51. For an interesting critique of Durkheim's version of evolution-

ary jurisprudence, see L. Sheleff, 'From restitutive law to repressive law', 1975.

52. On Lévi-Strauss's nostalgia, see T. O'Hagan, 'Rousseau, conservative or revolutionary?', 1978, pp. 31–3.
53. Page references in the text in this section are to A. Allott, *The Limits of Law*.
54. For the history of this process in the United States, see R. Dworkin, *Taking Rights Seriously*, in particular 'Constitutional Cases'.
55. I develop this theme in section 6.1 below.
56. J. Rawls, *A Theory of Justice*, 1972, p. 364.

2

Kant and Hegel

We begin our historical reflections with a brief comment on Kant's troubled attempts to come to terms with the phenomenon of legal individualism. We follow the development of that theme in the German tradition as it is elaborated by Hegel and Marx up to the point where the distinction between *Gemeinschaft* and *Gesellschaft* is crystallized by Tönnies. We note Pashukanis's isolated attempt to construct a full-scale jurisprudence out of Marx's asides on law and the market. Finally we use J. S. Mill's *On Liberty* as the source from which to plunder the elements of a model of liberal pluralism. As a historical narrative, it is far from comprehensive, ignoring both the French liberal tradition from Tocqueville[1] and the subsequent development of German social theory inaugurated by Max Weber.

2.1 KANT: AN UNHAPPY COMPROMISE

Kant's aim, in his *Rechtslehre* and in his other essays on law and political theory, was to construct a social model corresponding to the ideal of radical freedom which he had already espoused at the level of the individual in his moral philosophy. His problem was to embody in a socio-legal order the 'practical imperative': 'Act in such a way that you always treat humanity, whether in your own person or in the person of any other, never simply as a means, but always at the same time as an end'.[2]

In his essay on *The Conjectural Beginning of Human History* (1786)[3] Kant had applied the moral imperative to the political domain in a programmatic sketch of historical development leading to a point where

. . . man had entered into a relation of equality with all rational beings, whatever their rank, with respect to the claim of being an end in himself, respected as such by everyone, a being which no one might treat as a mere means to ulterior ends.

He went on to develop the idea of the interdependence of political freedom and political equality with an explicit acknowledgement to Rousseau's *Second Discourse* and its account of social inequality, not inequality as regards natural talent or worldly good fortune, but with regard to universal human rights:[4]

Surely nature did not intend this inequality, for she gave man freedom and along with it reason, by which to limit this freedom through nothing other than its own inherent conformity to law, a universal and external lawfulness which is called *civil right*.

Kant's commitment to the interdependence thesis continued into his essay on *Perpetual Peace* (1795)[5]

. . . my external and rightful *freedom* should be defined as a warrant to obey no external laws except those to which I have been able to give my own consent. Similarly, external and rightful *equality* within a state is that relationship among the citizens whereby no-one can put anyone else under a legal obligation without submitting simultaneously to a law which requires that he can himself be put under the same kind of obligation by the other person.

Indeed juridical egalitarianism can properly be seen as 'the fundamental principle of the Kantian conception of the *Rechtsstaat*'.[6] That principle runs through Kant's repeated criticisms of the residual corporations of the *ancien régime* and the continuation of feudal landed property. Against them Kant demanded the freedom of labour and of trade and the disposability of land.[7]

Yet, when he came to work out his political ideas in systematic form in his last major philosophical work, the *Rechtslehre* of 1796/7, Kant found himself lost in a maze of contradictions in attempting to give rational legal expression to the status of three categories of person: wives, children and domestic servants.[8] In the sections devoted to private law,

Kant began by describing the two standard rights of private law: real right (§§11–17)[9] as the right of possession of a material object, and personal right (§§18–21) as the right to exact services or other actions from another person, arising from contractual agreement: 'valid only to the effect of acting upon a particular physical person and specially upon the causality of his will, so that he shall perform something for me' (§20).

But in addition to these two standard rights, Kant proceeded to describe a third category, that of 'real-personal right' (§§22–30): Kant's own, unhappy innovation in legal theory.[10] This kind of right was to extend over wives, children and domestic servants, which are all 'acquired' as material objects are (§23) and which can be recovered by the master of the household if they run away or if (like a material object) they are appropriated by another. Kant's embarrassment in describing the master's 'real-personal right' over his wife and servants is signalled by the evasive 'as if':

> If one of the married persons run away or enter the possession of another, the other is entitled . . . to bring such a one back to the former relation, as if that person were a thing. (§25)
>
> . . . there is established a domestic relationship not founded on social equality, but such that one commands as master and another obeys as servant. The domestics or servants may then be regarded by the master of the household as thus far his. As regards the *form* or mode of his possession of them, they belong to him as if by a real right; for if any of them run away, he is entitled to bring them again under his power by a unilateral act of his will. (§30)

This 'real-personal right' is anomalous in Kant's system in that it denies the three properties which make a human being into a citizen, a subject of the *Rechtsstaat*: freedom, equality and personality. In the case of children, there is no problem in envisaging them as potential, though not yet full, bearers of rights,[11] but wives and servants are presumably rational adults. Why, then, was Kant driven to assign them to the juridical limbo of 'real-personal rights', midway between things and persons? The answer must be found in the primitive state of capitalist relations of Germany in 1796.

Kant's manoeuvres were a vain attempt to rationalize the remnants of feudal legal relations, based on 'personal' ties of dependence.

Legal equality was explicitly denied to servants and implicitly to wives, in so far as the 'real personal right' in marriage accrued only to the husband over the wife and not *vice versa*, since the husband, as master of the family, acquired the wife, who was thus passively acquired in the transaction. This legal inequality between the two parties determined the relation of freedom/unfreedom between them: the one party was entitled to act contrary to the will of the other and not *vice versa*. Most importantly, the subordinate party lacked full legal personality. The relation was contractual, in the sense that the subordinate was not to be treated as a thing, to be used or abused without constraint by the master. Yet it was a contract which effectively excluded the subordinate from participation in the *Rechtsstaat*, either as a political being or as an economic agent, able to dispose of his labour power without legal hindrance. The bizarrely literal application of the idea of contract to marriage as the 'union of two persons of different sex for life-long reciprocal possession of their sexual faculties' was continuous with Kant's advocacy of a pure *Gesellschaft*, the universalization of the two standard rights (real and personal) in pure abstraction. Hence the feudal privileges of the aristocracy and the Church were to be abolished and the Church's residual welfare functions ('to preserve those members of society who cannot do so for themselves' and to 'support . . . children abandoned through need or through shame', §49, General Remark C) were to be transferred to the state, which would thenceforth finance welfare institutions by taxation.

Thus Kant elaborated the formal categories of the *Rechtsstaat*, of the universe of property rights and legal freedom, where free, independent rights-bearers would exist over against the state, which, in the absence of feudal institutions, would become the sole guarantor of rights. But the attempt to universalize those categories foundered on the recalcitrant presence of relations of 'dépendance personelle': apparently banished for ever in Rousseau's *Social Contract*, but revived by Kant in the unhappy compromise of 'real-personal rights'. In this respect, Kant's *Rechtslehre* can be seen to contrast with Hegel's universalization of the category of subject of rights, his explicit exclusion of the family (wife and children) from the domain of contract and his rejection of all ties which could bind a worker to a master for life. Hegel was to adopt a full-scale juridical individualism which would involve him in serious theoretical problems at the political level. But he sought remedies for those problems in the realms of political education and political intervention, rather than in regression to anomalous legal forms.

2.2 HEGEL AND THE LAW: THE PROBLEM OF MEDIATIONS

Hegel's goal in the *Philosophy of Right* was to describe the political system which would allow the fullest expression of individual freedom. In order that this should not remain a mere abstract aspiration, 'a person must translate his freedom into an external sphere' (§41),[12] which meant 'putting his will into any and every thing and thereby making it his' (§44). Therefore a fully rational political system would be one which guaranteed the possibility of self-expression via the appropriation of external objects; and a fully rational legal system would be one which best codified that property system.

Hegel's account of law will be considered under four headings: the codification of law; the universalization of full legal freedom and equality; the abolition of dependency relations within the family; the problem of atomization.

The codification of law

Hegel supported the codification of law into an increasingly unified and rational system, consistently opposing the positivist upholders of customary law:[13] he reserved his particular animus for English law, which he attacked in philosophical[14] and political[15] writings. For Hegel, the English system was marred by two major defects: juridically, it lacked the 'scientific remodelling of law', making 'the constitution of England . . . a complex of mere *particular* rights and *particular* privileges';[16] and politically 'each particular church, parochial district . . . takes care of itself, so that the government, strictly speaking, has nowhere less to do than in England'.[17] For Hegel, it was self-evident that political centralization and juridical rationalization must accompany one another in the abolition of the remnants of feudalism. This judgement was particularly relevant to the fragmented world of early nineteenth century Germany, though for Hegel it formed part of a general thesis concerning the integration of freedom and rationality at all levels, in particular at the political and juridical levels.[18]

The universalization of full legal freedom and equality

For Hegel, progress towards full legal freedom and equality meant that there could be only one fundamental limitation on what could be alienated (bought and sold), namely human freedom itself (§66). Specifically, this meant that labour power could be alienated only for a restricted period (§67). Hegel thus finally broke with any remaining feudal obligations which could tie individuals beyond a temporally limited labour contract. The other side of this rejection of feudal survivals was the principle that all ownership was ownership in the full liberal sense:[19]

> If the whole and entire use of a thing were mine, while the abstract ownership were supposed to be someone else's then the thing as mine would be penetrated through and through by my will and at the same time there would remain in the thing something impenetrable by me, namely the . . . empty will of another . . . ownership therefore in essence is free and complete. (§62)

Hegel saw the emergence of 'free and complete' ownership as the most important result of centuries of juridical development,[20] though he did not attribute the advance to anything so vulgar as capitalism. He came near to doing so in the following Remark:[21]

> It is possible, in principle, to be the owner of a thing without at the same time being the owner of its value. If a family can neither sell nor pawn its goods, it is not the owner of their value. But since this

form of property is not in accordance with the concept of property, such restrictions on ownership (feudal tenure, testamentary trusts) are mostly in the course of disappearing. (Addition to §63, p. 240)

The abolition of dependency relations within the family

Hegel advocated the abolition of legally enforced dependency relations within the family. He saw it as a major defect of Roman law (at least in early times) that it regarded children on the same level as slaves to the paterfamilias. (There was more than a trace of that Roman conception in Kant's view that children are in the possession of, though not the property of, their parents.) For Hegel, 'children were potentially [*an sich*] free and embodied nothing save potential freedom' (§175) and in place of legal bonds he put education, designed to instil 'love, trust and obedience' (§175).

In the same spirit, Hegel excluded marriage from the domain of contract and attacked Kant for subsuming it under the concept of contract (§75):

> . . . marriage, so far as its essential basis is concerned, is not a contractual relation. On the contrary, though marriage begins in contract, it is precisely a contract to transcend the standpoint . . . from which persons are regarded in their individuality as self-subsistent units. The identification of personalities, whereby the family becomes one person and its members become accidents . . . is the ethical mind. (§163)

This argument was a curious one, because every contract which resulted in incorporation, i.e. the production of a new legal person (company, university etc.) had the effect of endowing the parties, *qua* members of the corporation, with a new status (directors, shareholders, fellows etc.). One is tempted to think that Hegel was seeking to rationalize a growing economic individualism, such that families, lacking a substantive economic function *qua* unit of production would be held together, if at all, by some higher 'standpoint', even though they would still maintain the economic role of the transmission of the family capital or estate (*Vermögen*):

> The family, as a person, has its real external existence in property; and it is only when this property takes the form of capital [*Vermögen*]

that it becomes the embodiment of the substantive personality of the family. (§169)

As such, it needed a legal representative, a role which Hegel saw accruing 'naturally' to the husband.

The problem of atomization

Hegel's belief in the necessity of 'free and complete' ownership, his opposition to trusts and his general advocacy of legal individualism in the family ('the principle that the members of the family grow up to be self-subsistent persons in the eyes of the law') would all seem to have tended to the 'injury of the basic family relationship' (§180), in other words to undermining the family as the central unit of social and economic cohesion. To prevent this, Hegel put a major legal limit on the freedom to dispose of property, in the sphere of testamentary disposition, in order to preserve the estate within the family (§180). Once again Hegel attacked the freedom of disposition 'prevalent in England, the home of all sorts of eccentricity, where there is no end to the folly and whimsicality of bequests' (Addition to §180, p. 266). But he provided no philosophical justification for restricting one of the central incidents of property[22] within a system which was claimed to embody 'free and complete' ownership.

Individualism within the family was only one aspect of the general process of political and social atomization inaugurated by capitalism. Hegel viewed the process with great anxiety and sought measures to mitigate its effects at every level. His anticipation of later *Gemeinschaft* theorists was in this respect remarkable. It was a mark of his intellectual rigour that he nowhere tried to collapse the sphere of abstract right, for all its dangerous atomistic tendencies, into that of ethical life, as later theorists were tempted to do. The tensions and conflicts between atomization and *Gemeinschaft* remained unresolved to the conclusion of the *Philosophy of Right*, despite Hegel's aim of bringing about their dialectical *Aufhebung* in the state.

Hegel's vision of the negative effects of .contemporary society was of a juxtaposition of isolated citizens on the one hand and of a state machine on the other, without any mediating organs through which individuals could effectively express their freedom. Hegel saw two striking models of that atomization:

(1) The model of the Roman Empire

in which all individuals are degraded to the level of private persons, equal with one another, possessed of formal rights and the only bond left to hold them together is abstract, inalienable self-will. (§357)

(2) The model of the French Revolution as heralded by Rousseau's general will, in which 'fanaticism wills an abstraction' and the

revolutionaries destroyed once more the institutions which they had made themselves, since any institution whatever is antagonistic to the abstract self-consciousness of equality. (Addition to §5, pp. 227–8)

Much of Hegel's effort in the *Philosophy of Right* was devoted to seeking the mediations which would allow freedom and individuality to flourish without yielding atomization and alienation.[23]

Hegel attempted to harmonize the need for individualism on the one hand, and the need for solidarity and communal activity on the other, at many levels, including that of the 'corporations' in civil society. Hegel envisaged that these intermediate organs would integrate the necessarily individualistic, egotistical and centrifugal lives of the members of the 'business class', the class which was 'essentially concentrated on the particular' (§250).

The curious feature of these bodies (a feature which re-emerged in the later *Gemeinschaft* theories) is the nostalgia they represent for medieval craft guilds, the embodiment of craft skill and craft loyalty in an economic system where crafts were already dead or dying.[24] For Hegel, the corporations would be exclusive, open to the 'master of his craft', not to 'a day-labourer or . . . a man who is prepared to undertake casual employment on a single occasion' (§252). As such a corporation would combine the following functions:

. . . to look after its own interests within its own sphere, to co-opt members, qualified objectively by the requisite skill and rectitude, to a number fixed by the general structure of society, to protect its members against particular contingencies, to provide the education requisite to fit others to become members. In short, its right is to come on the scene like a second family for its members. (§252)

The corporation would thus provide training, qualifications and insurance and, psychologically, a concrete status for its members, an unchanging identity in an increasingly anonymous and unstable social system:

In addition, this nexus of capability and livelihood is a recognized fact, with the result that the Corporation member needs no external marks beyond his own membership as evidence of his skill and his regular income and subsistence, i.e. as evidence that he is a somebody. It is also recognized that he belongs to a whole which is itself an organ of the entire society, and that he is actively concerned in promoting the comparatively disinterested end of this whole. Thus he commands the respect due to one in his social position. (§253)

The corporations then could have had an important, if hazily defined, role to play in overcoming the atomization of certain – but only certain – members of society. For those whom Hegel labelled 'day-labourers', no such mediating bodies were envisaged. For them, life was to be supported by the alienation to their employers of 'single products of [their] particular physical and mental skill . . . the use of [their] abilities for a restricted period' (§67). For me to alienate something is to express 'my will no longer to regard the thing as mine' (§65A). The 'day-labourer' therefore, must have regarded his 'particular physical and mental skill' as no longer his, as long as he was working, and thus must have been condemned to enjoy only abstract rights, to which no positive external expression was given. Hegel recognized how dangerously close he thus came to categorizing the 'day-labourer's' life as slavery, or even worse than ancient slavery, in so far as the 'Athenian slave perhaps had an easier occupation and more intellectual work than is usually the case with our servants' (§67A). But the legal difference between the two remained, that the 'day-labourer', unlike the slave, retained legal personality, the legal right (however narrowly economically circumscribed) to withdraw his labour power, or transfer it to another employer.

'Day-labourers', then, in Hegel's system, were legally free, but without any *Gemeinschaft* to integrate them and mediate their atomized isolation. The 'poor' in particular, in Hegel's system, had nothing to mediate between their powerless isolation and the draconian 'welfare' system to which they were subjected, since the family had been destroyed as a productive unit, while the corporations acted as surrogate families only to the business class (§241).

It might be argued that Hegel attributed the ultimate mediating role to the state itself envisaging that at the highest political level, the supposed synthesis between particular and individual interests, the 'actuality of concrete freedom' (§260) would be realized. In this sense, since freedom, for Hegel, demanded concrete expression, recognition and security for the free individual as subject of rights and owner of property, and since the 'day-labourer's' restricted freedom stemmed from his lack of property, the relation of the state to the property system was a crucial but apparently insoluble problem for Hegel:

> The *rational* aspect is that I possess property . . . what and how much I possess is . . . a matter of chance so far as rights are concerned ['eine rechtliche Zufälligkeit']. (§49)

> The principle that a thing belongs to the person who happens to be first in time to take it into his possession ['dem in der Zeit zufällig Ersten, der sic in Besitz nimmt'] is immediately self-explanatory and superfluous, because a second person cannot take into his possession what is already the property of another. (§50)

So, for Hegel, chance ultimately decided both the quantity of property an individual owned and the distribution of property to sets of individuals, based on a title traced back to the traditional fiction of chance occupancy of a *res nullius*. Given that a system based on chance and contingency was an irrational system for Hegel and that reason was the key to spiritual progress, the base of the political order seems to have lain wholly beyond rational control for him. In this sense, the political order ultimately shared the 'impotence of Nature', in contrast with the strength of *Geist*, since, like Nature, it failed to overcome 'contingency and determination from without . . . in the realm of concrete individual forms' (*PN*, §250).[25]

But if Hegel regarded the fundamental distribution of property as lying outside the concern of the law, it might be argued that he made it subject to rational control at other levels. Thus Marcuse defended Hegel's legal abstraction in the following terms:[26]

> This insight into the material connection between the rule of law and the rule of property compels Hegel . . . to go beyond the liberalist doctrine. Because of this connection, the law cannot be the final point of integration for civil society, nor can it represent its real universality. The rule of law merely embodies the 'abstract right' of property. . . . The law must therefore be supplemented and even supplanted by a much stronger and stricter force which will govern individuals more directly and more visibly.

But this 'stronger and stricter force' (the 'police' and 'corporations' at the level of civil society and the state machine at the political level) turned out to be powerless, within the terms of Hegel's own theory, to do more than mitigate some of the worst effects of the underlying property relation. Legal abstraction established that, as far as the law is concerned, only the equal right of all to property is established; not the right of all to equal property or even the right of all to enough for subsistence. But 'subsistence is not the same as possession and belongs to another sphere, i.e. to civil society' (§49).

But when we reach civil society we find a full barrage of accidental factors recognized. At §195 we discover that in the actual process of production

> . . . dependence and want increase *ad infinitum* and the material to meet these is permanently barred to the needy man because it consists of external objects with the special character of being property.

Given the vagueness of Hegel's terminology at this point, in particular the unspecific reference to 'the needy man', it is unclear what proportion of the population he envisaged in 'dependence and want' who were 'permanently barred' from improving their lot. He clearly saw that this situation was a function of the distribution of property, since the needy man's barrier is precisely the rich man's property; 'the embodiment of the free will of others', so that 'from his point of view its recalcitrance is absolute'.

Anyway, whatever the size of the 'needy' class, it emerges at §200 that the whole of a man's chances in life lay outside the domain of reason and organization:

> A particular man's resources, or in other words his opportunity of sharing in the general resources are conditioned . . . *partly by . . . his own unearned . . . capital* and partly by his skill; this in turn is itself dependent not only on his capital but also on accidental circumstances whose multiplicity introduces differences of natural, bodily and mental characteristics.

So, at the fundamental level of distribution of resources in society, Hegel rendered his political system impotent. His mediating organs (the 'corporations') turned out to have a welfare function restricted to their own members (the business class), while the state was condemned by virtue of its legal abstraction to a role of non-intervention in the property system, except as the legal guarantor of established property rights.

In his *Philosophy of Right* Hegel nonetheless raised, in a striking form, a set of problems which were to remain central for later social theory. First, he most clearly delineated the modern *Rechtsstaat* as a system of legally assertable and enforceable rights, backed by organized state power, a power which was itself constitutionally limited. Second, with his acute consciousness of social change, particularly within the family, he anticipated later discussions of individualism and atomization. Third, in his hesitant moves beyond the pure abstraction of the Kantian *Rechtsstaat,* he anticipated the problem of theorizing the passage from a non-interventionist to an interventionist state. Hegel anticipated Marx with his insight into the connection between freedom and property, but held back from giving reality to that connection, from giving a content to the abstract *Rechtsstaat.*

NOTES

1. For the French tradition see L. Siedentop, 'Two liberal traditions', 1979.
2. I. Kant, *The Moral Law,* 1965 edition, p. 96.
3. I. Kant, *On History,* 1963 edition, p. 59. In this and the previous passage, Kant leaves himself a formal escape in the qualifications 'simply as a means', 'a mere means'. But it is hard to see how those qualifications could be made more specific without devaluing the means/end distinction altogether.
4. Ibid., p. 62.
5. I. Kant, *Kant's Political Writings,* 1971 edition, p. 99.
6. G. Vlachos, *La Pensée Politique de Kant,* 1962, p. 380.
7. I. Kant, *Rechtslehre,* 1968 edition, §§49, 88, and Additional Remark 8. See G. Vlachos, *La Pensée Politique de Kant,* pp. 381–5, for discussion of these passages.
8. See especially B. Edelman, 'Transitions in Kant's *The Metaphysical Elements of Justice*' in *The Ownership of the Image,* 1979, Appendix 2.
9. Paragraph references in this section are to I. Kant, *Rechtslehre.*
10. B. Edelman, *The Ownership of the Image,* pp. 151–3.
11. 'From the fact of personality of children . . . they can never be regarded as the property [*Eigentum*] of the parents, but only as belonging to them as by way of being in their *possession* [*Besitz*], like other things that are held apart from possession of all others and that can be brought back even against the will of the subjects.' (§29)
12. Unless otherwise specified, all paragraph references in this section are to G. W. F. Hegel, *Philosophy of Right,* 1942 edition.
13. See especially §211 and Addition to §211, pp. 136–7.
14. Ibid. and *PH,* p. 474. (For abbreviations used to refer to Hegel's texts, see Bibliography).
15. *PW,* p. 300.
16. *PH,* p. 474.
17. Ibid.
18. Though it is arguable that in seventeenth century England progress towards capitalism and the destruction of feudal ties was facilitated precisely by the *absence* of political and legal centralization. (See C. Hill, *Reformation to Industrial Revolution,* 1969, p. 95).
19. See A. Honoré, 'Ownership' 1961, p. 110.
20. 'It is about a millenium and a half since the freedom of personality began through the spread of Christianity to blossom and gain recognition as a universal principle from a part, though

still a small part, of the human race. But it was only yesterday, we might say, that the principle of the freedom of property became recognized in some places. This example from history may serve to rebuke the impatience of opinion and to show the length of time that mind requires for progress in its self-consciousness.' (§62)

21. A rash prediction, in the light of the flourishing state of trust law in Anglo-Saxon countries. Though Hegel might simply have attributed this phenomenon to the irrationality ('eccentricity') of English law.
22. See A. Honoré, 'Ownership', pp. 120–1.
23. Discussed in G. Heiman, 'The sources and significance of Hegel's corporate doctrine', 1971.
24. See the note by A. Gramsci, *Selections from the Prison Notebooks*, 1971 edition, p. 259: 'Hegel, in a certain sense, . . . already transcended pure constitutionalism and theorised the parliamentary State with its party system. But his conception of association could not help still being vague and primitive, halfway between the political and the economic; it was in accordance with the historical experience of the time, which was very limited and offered only one perfected example of organisation – the "corporative" (a politics grafted directly on to the economy).'
25. It is instructive to compare Hegel's attitude to the role of chance in the capitalist economic system with that of Marx and Engels. The latter agreed, naturally, that the specific quantity of property accumulated by an *individual* in a capitalist system is a matter of chance. But for them, that distribution was contained within closely defined limits, necessary parts of the system as a whole, determining the accumulation of property at the level of *classes*. These limits were the monopolization of ownership of the means of production by the capitalist class and the incapacity of the proletarian class to accumulate capital to the extent that it became independent of wage-labour in order to reproduce itself. Thus the system allowed for individuals who by chance (lottery, pools, self-made capitalist, etc.) managed to cross the class lines, but it would be overthrown if the working class as a whole could do so. So, while at the level of the individual 'what and how much I own is a matter of chance so far as rights are concerned', distribution at the level of classes was not a matter of chance, relative to the economic system: equally, that distribution could be altered by political and legal action.
26. H. Marcuse, *Reason and Revolution*, 1969 edition, p. 210.

3

Marxism and the *Rechtsstaat*

3.1 MARX'S FLIRTATION WITH *GEMEINSCHAFTLICHKEIT*

> In [Marx], and in Engels too, there is a strong nostalgic streak which makes them always a little tender of archaic societies in which money is not dominant . . .
>
> Lionel Trilling, *Sincerity and Authenticity*

It is well known that Marx shunned explicit normative advocacy of a concrete type of social order to replace the present one. The polemics against the utopian and other brands of idealist socialists in the *Manifesto* are continuous with the ideology of 'scientific socialism' and the ambivalent approach to the fact/value distinction inherited from the Hegelian dialectic.[1] Yet there are certain implicit normative themes in Marx's writing, in particular the dialectical flirtation with *Gemeinschaftlichkeit* present both in the essay *On The Jewish Question* (1843) and in the *Grundrisse* (1857).[2]

On the Jewish Question

For the young Marx, the *Rechtsstaat* was the world of contingency and egotism, the world of private property, in which social relations were fragmented and atomized. From this perspective Marx discussed the process of Germany's 'political emancipation from religion', the process of banishing religion from the public to the private domain and the legal form of that transformation.[3] Marx characterized it as 'a great step forward' ('ein grosser Fortschritt'), as 'the last form of human emancipation within the previous world order', but not 'the last form of emancipation altogether' (*CW*, 3, p. 155, Kröner, p. 183).[4] Marx said of religion when it was relegated to the private sphere that it 'no longer embodied community' ('nicht mehr das Wesen der Gemeinschaft'), but now 'embodied difference' ('das Wesen des Unterschieds'), 'the expression of man's separation from his communal being' ('Ausdruck der Trennung des Menschen von seinem Gemeinwesen'): the suggestion being that religion once embodied that lost community, which is yet to be regained. Throughout the text Marx stressed the fragmentation (*Zersplitterung*), splitting (*Splattung*) and isolation–individualization (*Absonderung*) of present day society. More explicitly than in later texts he advocated a way out of this unhappy state for the individual, as he 're-absorbed in himself ['in sich zurücknimmt'] the abstract citizen' (*CW*, 3, p. 168, Kröner, p. 199).

This normative claim has been noted by two recent commentators, Kolakowski[5] and Keat.[6] Kolakowski saw Marx's advocacy as part of a general utopian programme, expressing a yearning for a realm of social integration – 'as it originally was' ('wie sie ursprünglich war'), in which civil and political society, the public and the private, could be reunited. Keat preferred to extract a more nuanced, differentiated model of the future order:

> . . . a unity [in which] there may still be an important role for institutions with 'separate' or distinct *functions*; but they will no longer be 'separate' in the principles and rights they embody. (LRS, pp. 79–80)

Those interested in the conditions necessary for the defence of civil liberties should be wary of the transformation of separate 'principles and rights' into separate 'functions'. If the distinction is more than empty rhetoric, it would seem to point to the instrumental-technical model of social regulation, in which the independent judiciary, capable of recognizing and defending citizens' rights against the executive, would be reduced to something analogous to a branch of an enterprise with a distinct function, but no ultimate autonomy.[7] But if constitutionality is a value to be defended in any future order, then it will still depend on a real separation between the judicial and the political in the *Rechtsstaat*, a distribution of 'principles and rights' to different natural and legal persons.[8] Thus the possibility of conflict between asserted rights and the means of recognizing and enforcing those rights by authoritative adjudication is inscribed in the form of the *Rechtsstaat*. No 'dialectical' syntheses will 'supersede' the opposition between that form and the form of substantively consensual *Gemeinschaft*.

If 'separation' (*Absonderung*) is an irreducible form of the *Rechtsstaat* at the level of administrative organs, it is equally so at the level of the individual. Particular individuals may integrate their roles as family member, voter, employee, etc. more or less successfully, but there is no reason to think that such a multiplicity of roles will or should be transformed in a dialectical synthesis: in complex societies, there is every reason to think that individual citizens will want to continue to protect their separation with the fragile armour of constitutionally enforceable civil liberties. At this level too, the yearning for 're-absorption' should be viewed with scepticism.

The Grundrisse

The *Grundrisse*, Marx's fragmentary, unpublished notebooks of 1857, cannot be read as a definitive statement of his views on any topic. Yet, in so far as they contain some of his most extended reflections on the law, their unfinished state may indicate that not only lack of time, but also theoretical obstacles, forced Marx into reaching such oblique and elusive formulations. There is a clear continuity between the 1843/4 *Manuscripts* and the 1857 Notebooks in the theme of community and the critique of the *Rechtsstaat* for its failure to embody *gemeinschaftlich* values. The later text differs from the former in locating the theme more firmly in an historical context. Typical *Grundrisse* asides on the law are the following:

> Equality and freedom presuppose relations of production as yet unrealized in the ancient world and in the Middle Ages. (*G*, p. 245)

> . . . insofar as it [Roman Law] was developed in a limited sphere, it was able to develop the *attributes of the juridical person, precisely of the individual engaged in exchange*, and thus anticipate (in its basic aspects) the legal relations of industrial society, and in particular the

right which rising bourgeois society had necessarily to assert against medieval society. (*G*, p. 246)

. . . this presupposition by no means arises either out of the individual's will or out of the immediate nature of the individual, but . . . it is, rather, *historical*, and posits the individual as already *determined* by society. (*G*, p. 248)

The thesis is that the distribution of legal freedom and equality to all citizens 'presupposes' a particular economic form, namely capitalism; that it 'presupposes' in particular the relations of exchange between buyers and sellers of labour power. This legal freedom and equality not only coexists with economic inequality, i.e. a relation of unequal power between the classes, it 'presupposes' that relation. Legal relations then embody relations of formal equality and independence, but substantive inequality and dependence:

As far as the formal character is concerned, there is absolutely no distinction between them, and this is the economic character, the aspect in which they stand towards one another in the exchange relation; it is the indicator of their social function or social relation towards one another. Each of the subjects is an exchanger; i.e. each has the same social relation towards the other that the other has towards him. As subjects of exchange, their relation is therefore that of *equality*. (*G*, p. 241)

These formal properties are seen as illusory, but illusory in a particular sense:

. . . individuals *seem* independent (this is an independence which is at bottom merely an illusion, and it is more correctly called indifference), free to collide with one another and to engage in exchange within this freedom; but they appear thus only for someone who abstracts from the *conditions*, the *conditions of existence* within which these individuals enter into contract. (*G*, pp. 163–4)

Marx argued that capitalist law embodied an illusion, the illusion that, with the passing of feudalism, personal ties were replaced by real independence for individuals. In reality, Marx suggested, the personal ties were replaced only by relations of 'indifference', allowing individuals the 'freedom to collide'. What was illusory, according to Marx, was not the abolition of personal ties, but the effect of that abolition:

> Both sides confront each other as persons. *Formally,* their relation has the equality and freedom of exchange as such. As far as concerns the legal relation, the fact that this form is a mere *semblance*, and a *deceptive semblance,* appears as an *external* matter. (*G*, p. 464)

The charges of 'indifference' and 'illusion' need to be examined, as they cover a number of different features which Marx saw as characteristic of the *Rechtsstaat*.

First, Marx saw the law as being 'indifferent' in the sense that it remained external to questions of economic power. Inverting the Hegelian relation of form and content, Marx saw the law as 'indifferent' to the content, the essence, the basis of social life, just as Hegel had seen it as properly 'indifferent' to matters which were accidental and contingent.

Second, Marx assumed that in the world of legal persons no legal distinctions could be drawn which corresponded to the real differences between employer and employee, merchant and customer, etc.:

> As far as the formal character is concerned, there is absolutely no distinction between them . . . each has the same social relation to the other as the other has towards him. (*G*, p. 241)

But since the two parties in each case occupy different positions in the power structure, that 'indifference' must be a sham.[9]

Third, Marx historicized the account of 'indifference' by use of the schema of 'presuppositions': 'the exchange of exchange values is the productive, real basis of all *equality* and *freedom*'. The latter are 'merely idealized expressions of this capitalist basis' and 'presuppose capitalist relations of production'. In these condensed comments, Marx combined the correct historical thesis that the passage to capitalism is the necessary condition for universalizing legal freedom and equality with the normative suggestion, in the phrase 'merely idealized expression', that the latter are unreal and transitory.

We shall return to this third theme in section 3.3. Anticipating its conclusions, we can say that a modest and defensible version of Marxist historicism does not proceed from the premiss that capitalism had universalized the values of the *Rechtsstaat* to the conclusion that those values are destined to be marginalized or transcended-surpassed as capitalism is transformed.

The first two charges assert that the law performs the twin functions of mystification and reinforcing the status quo in virtue of its abstraction-indifference towards relevant differences, so that workers are seen as being deluded by the apparent impartiality of the law into overlooking underlying inequalities of power. In its extreme form, this criticism is perhaps applicable only to the era of formalistic jurisprudence characteristic of *laissez-faire* economic policy. Post-liberal law, in contrast, has shown itself capable of recognizing relevant 'differences' ignored by formalism, in so far as formalism asserts the qualitative identity of all legal persons, whether individual natural persons (customers, workers, etc.) or artificial persons (corporations, government agencies, etc.). With the advent of welfare economics, when 'the state becomes involved in the tasks of overt redistribution, regulation and planning',[10] the abstraction of the law is modified. A typical example is the development of laws relating to freedom of information on the one hand and to personal privacy on the other. Here, as Michael has pointed out,[11] there are laws which 'treat information about people and information about companies as being essentially the same', yet increasingly 'data protection laws in most countries recognize that the privacy of a natural person is fundamentally different from that of a legal person'. Equally striking in their lack of abstraction are the codes of the great European documents, e.g. the Codes of the European Coal and Steel Community (1951) and of the European Economic Community (1957), which refer to the 'wages and movement of workers' (ECSC Art. 68), the 'freedom of movement of workers', 'equal pay without discrimination based on sex' (EEC Art. 48, 119). Tory resistance to that last provision is hardly surprising.[12] Post-war constitutions, most clearly the Italian, have specifically and concretely itemized workers' rights (Art. 36, 37), including the right to strike (Art. 40) and corporations' duties (Art. 42), albeit in 'programmatic', rather than 'preceptive' form.[13]

Within particular jurisdictions, from early times, the absolute abstract freedom of contract has been repeatedly modified in response to economic and political pressure:[14]

> The law of the late Roman Empire was faced with a situation in which powerful landowners could put almost intolerable economic pressure on smallholders who were reluctant to sell their land to them. The law's reaction to this state of affairs was the rule known as *laesio enormis*: such a sale would be upheld only if the buyer made up the price to what the court considered a just price.

Such limitations have, naturally, aroused the hostility of those who object that 'the law is making the contract for the parties instead of allowing them to make it themselves . . . challenging their position as individuals'. But, as Stein and Shand have pointed out, civil law systems such as French law have had no difficulty in incorporating this degree of paternalism, which makes it impossible for individuals 'to bind themselves as they are ready to do, if the result is too damaging to their interests'. From the rather distant perspective of left critics of welfarism, such developments must be merely cosmetic, since 'the revolution' is something which bypasses legal forms in direct action. My own views of the shift of power between classes is rather different, since I envisage the law as both an instrument of change and the form of any new order. From a perspective closer to the law itself it is impossible in the post-liberal era to assert that there is a necessary connection between capitalism and legal formalism as envisaged in the *Grundrisse*.

In short, the *Grundrisse's* model of the counter-order is close to that of 1843, though clad in more explicitly dialectical clothing. Marx saw juridical independence and equality as 'preferable' to feudal bondage, but itself ripe for *Aufhebung* (*G*, p. 161). He rejected the nostalgic 'yearning for return' (*Zurücksehnen*), but equally the conservative contentment with the present order (*G*, p. 162). But once again, the counter-order is not simply one which makes concrete the freedom and equality of the present one, but one which is qualitatively transformed: 'a communal production, communality' (*Gemeinschaftlichkeit*) (*G*, p. 172. Gmn., p. 88). In place of the contingency and indifference of capitalism, it is 'the social conditions within which the individual is active' that are made primary.

The rejection of the *Rechtsstaat,* implicit in oblique form in both *On the Jewish Question* and the *Grundrisse* is made explicit in the *German Ideology,* in which Marx and Engels claimed that they and others had

> ... stressed the opposition of communism to law [*Recht*] both political and private, as also in its general form as the rights of man.

In contrast to the dialectical subtleties of the more Hegelian texts, in the *German Ideology* they resorted to a straightforward functionalism: the law (*Recht*) is 'something corresponding to the state of competition, of free, private property' (*CW,* 5, p. 209. *W,* 3, p. 190). Thus 'the opposition of communism to law' was simply an extension of its opposition to the economic system to which it 'corresponded'. But whether Marx's model of 'correspondence' licenses such an extension is, as we shall see later in the chapter, questionable.

3.2 A MARXIST THEORY OF LAW?

Legal Progress

In his early writings, Marx followed Hegel in attacking the school of legal positivists. Marx criticized this school for justifying any legal system in place by its particular brand of functionalism:[15] if it was in place, then presumably it served the function of maintaining order satisfactorily in the given circumstances. When this doctrine was applied to contemporary legal institutions, it involved a complete conservatism, in that

> ... it justifies the infamy of today by the infamy of yesterday ... history shows only its *a posteriori,* as did the God of Israel to his servant Moses. (Introduction to *Contribution to Critique of Hegel's Philosophy of Right CW*, 3, p. 177)[16]

In this early text, Marx was talking in abstract terms about the emergence of reason in law without providing very concrete criteria for judging progress in legal rationality. When in their later texts he and Engels attempted to connect juridical and productive relations, they did not abandon the view that it is possible to observe progress in legal systems, but now adopted a more elaborate functionalist criterion for judging that progress: namely, how well does a particular legal system facilitate the reproduction and development of the relations of that mode of production and, in particular, how well does it allow for their transformation? That is the unifying theme of their scattered comments on legal progress, detached from the *gemeinschaftlich* nostalgia of the *Manuscripts* and the *Grundrisse* discussed above. It constitutes, I think, their most positive contribution to legal theory.

Marx and Engels saw modern law as more rational than its predecessors in at least three respects:

(1) At the level of commercial law, Engels was particularly insistent that the French *Code Civil* was the best adapted to the task of furthering commercial transactions, and thereby the development of the productive forces.[17] In his *Origin of the Family*, Engels produced a complex account of the rhythm of the induction of further groups of people, notably women, into the labour force, and the corresponding demand by them for equal legal status, which became irresistible.[18]

(2) At the level of fundamental legal categories, they saw the universalization of the category of free subject of rights as the outcome of the universalization in Western Europe of capitalist relations. Only capitalism makes everyone into a potential exchanger, as owner either of capital or labour power at the fundamental level, and thus only capitalism can effect this universalization: hence the spread of legal freedom and equality in the Roman Empire, as a result of its commercial development, but the continued exclusion of large sections of the population because of its continued reliance on slaves.[19]

(3) At the level of consciousness they saw the breaking of feudal ties, the residual bonds of personal dependence, as an essential part of the process whereby the labour force gains class consciousness. It enables the labourer to free himself from his 'definedness' (*Bestimmtheit*),[20] to see himself as a

member of a universal class. It enables him to 'relate himself' in a relatively active fashion to his environment, in the sense that he has freedom (at least legal freedom) to work for whom he pleases.[21] Further, it provides a critical standard for assessing economic inequality against the formality of legal equality.

Capitalist and Pre-capitalist Law

Introduction

Marx and Engels, were believers in progress in law as much as in other domains. As far as law is concerned, they shared the view held by Maine, Durkheim and others that 'the general movement of legal historical change was from an emphasis on legal community to an emphasis on legal individuality'.[22] They shared with Maine in particular the view that:[23]

> . . . society in primitive times was not what it is assumed to be at present, a collection of individuals. In fact, and in the view of the men who composed it, it was an *aggregation of families* . . . the *unit* of an ancient society was the Family, of a modern society, the Individual.

Associated with this social movement towards individualism, Maine traced 'the movement of the progressive societies . . . *from status to contract*'.[24]

Engels commented,[25] unfairly, that Maine 'believed that he had made a colossal discovery' in the formula '*from status to contract*', whereas in fact he was merely repeating an insight which 'insofar as it is correct was contained long ago in the *Communist Manifesto*'. Engels despised Maine's work because the latter failed to trace the source of the legal transformation to 'capitalist production', which

> . . . by transforming all things into commodities, . . . dissolved all ancient traditional relations, and for inherited customs and historical rights . . . substituted purchase and sale, 'free' contract.

Yet Maine's pioneering work on the evolution of legal categories must provide important theoretical and historical insights for anyone attempting to produce a serious materialist theory of law; and if Maine did not make the precise correlations with economic development that Marx and Engels did, his work is still quite consistent with them. Both his general thesis concerning progress towards individualism and his particular thesis concerning the development 'from status to contract' are implicit in most of their remarks on law.

Marx and Engels then shared the general 'progressive' view of law of nineteenth century evolutionary sociology. What gives their analyses a certain bite, relative to that of their contemporaries, is precisely their lack of interest in the law, as such. Just because they were primarily concerned with extra-legal social phenomena (economic, political) their treatment of law was patchy and avoided any overriding historicist assumption that progress towards rational, individualistic law is a universal, self-generating process.

The development of law, according to them, is dependent on the development of extra-legal relations: the uneven development of these latter relations on the Marxist account, is mirrored, frequently in a distorting mirror, by the uneven development of the former.[26]

But, however irregular, uneven and lacking in rational planning, the progressive evolution of legal systems is no illusion for Marx and Engels. In reflecting (usually *en passant*) on the relation between capitalist and pre-capitalist law Marx and Engels seem to have maintained two things: that where capitalist relations appear, certain transformations of legal relations follow and that the conjunction of a set of juridical categories cannot appear without capitalism. This is a conjunction of three clusters of categories:

(1) Legal equality and personality; the substitution of contract for status.

(2) The citizen as the subject of legal rights; the extension of property rights to their fullest extent.

(3) The bearer of rights as an individual legally responsible for his actions; tendency to abandon categories inconsistent with that, e.g. strict liability and vicarious liability.

There is every reason to think that Marx and Engels were right both in their evolutionary picture and in the explanatory account they gave of the connection between the development of capitalist production relations and the development of legal categories. In the following pages, I shall suggest that these categories are not found together, forming an interlocking system, in pre-capitalist law. My procedure will be either to point to the absence of one or more of the listed categories in a particular pre-capitalist legal system or to the presence of a category incompatible with a listed category, or, where there is the residual presence of a pre-capitalist category (one incompatible with a listed category), I shall point to the tendency of modern law, as it develops, to eliminate it (a tendency which is, however, never smooth or free from contradiction).

Legal equality: the substitution of contract for status

Marx's central historical concern in *Capital* was the transition from feudalism to capitalism; and it is in order to distinguish the two modes of production that he made some of his most complex distinctions in historical materialism. In the same way, in the realm of law, it is often in order to mark it off from feudalism that Marx characteristically stressed the levelling effect of capitalism. He contrasted, for instance, 'individuals imprisoned within a certain definition, as feudal lord and vassal' with those 'in the money relation, in the developed system of exchange . . . [when] the ties of personal dependence . . . are . . . exploded, ripped up . . .' (*G*, pp. 163–5). But in its role as leveller of juridical distinctions, Marx and Engels saw capitalism as contrasting with all pre-capitalist legal systems, including even Roman law, which, although it came to endow all free men with 'the attributes of the juridical person, precisely of the individual engaged in exchange, and thus anticipate (in its basic form) the legal relations of industrial society', nevertheless excluded a large part of the population from the legal universe, namely the slave, who was 'correctly defined as one who may not enter into exchange for the purpose of acquiring for himself . . .' (*G*, pp. 245–6). Since only capitalism demands a complete universe of exchangers (on the one hand those offering labour-power and on the other hand those offering wages) only capitalism produces a complete universe of legally free individuals, tied only by contract (*G*, p. 245, *AD*, pp. 142–3). The distinction between the forms of legal agreement typical of the pre-capitalist and capitalist systems was summarized by Weber as follows:[27]

The distinction is based on the fact that all those primitive contracts . . . involve a change in what may be called the total legal situation (the universal position) and the social status of the persons involved . . . By means of such a contract a person was to become somebody's child, father, wife, brother, master, slave, kin, comrade-in-arms, protector, client, follower, vassal, subject, friend, or, quite generally, comrade. . . . it meant that the person would 'become' something different in quality (or status) from the quality he possessed before.

Property

If legal ownership is, as Honoré defined it, 'the greatest possible interest in a thing which a mature system of law recognizes',[28] this definition is universally applicable in the sense that:[29]

. . . certain important legal incidents are found, which are common to different systems . . . Everywhere, the 'owner' can, in the simple, uncomplicated case, in which no other person has an interest in the thing, use it, stop others using it, lend it, sell it, or leave it by will.

But, observed Honoré (and this is the point where juridical and political theory meet), this does not mean that:[30]

. . . all systems attach an equal importance to ownership (in the full, liberal sense) or regard the same things as capable of being owned.

Honoré proceeded to list 11 'incidents of ownership',[31] starting from the basic 'right to possess', which includes both the possessor's right to remain undisturbed in possession and his right to recover possessions which have been removed from him.[32] The incidents include one prohibition, the 'prohibition of harmful use',[33] which Honoré saw as an essential part of any property system; the concept of ownership as an 'absolute' right allowing the owner 'to do anything he likes with the thing'[34] is simply unthinkable. It also includes a liability, the 'liability to execution' (allowing 'the owner's interest to be taken away from him for debt').[35]

Using Honoré's distinction, we can see that, in different systems, the extent to which private property is recognized may differ with respect to two different factors:

(1) With respect to the kinds of thing which can be owned within that system: e.g. consumer goods, houses, means of production, capital, dividends, shares, slaves, etc.
(2) With respect to the incidents of ownership recognized within that system: a system which does not protect the actual personal possession of any objects would not recognize private property at all; whereas a system which recognizes personal possession of certain material objects (and perhaps certain other incidents) but fails to recognize, for example, transmissibility (inheritance), does constitute a system of private property, though a more limited one than another system which recognizes transmissibility in addition to those other incidents.

Capitalism has provided a sharper impetus than any other mode of production to the extension of private property rights on three fronts:

(1) It has allowed the concentration of a maximum number of incidents of ownership on one person: i.e. it has vested a maximum number of legal powers (alienation, management, transmission, etc.) on a single individual.

(2) It has extended the range of kinds of thing that can be legally owned in two ways:

(a) It has made available for private ownership items which, although they existed in other productive systems, were excluded by them from private ownership. A striking example here is land: Marx contrasted the absence of important legal incidents (e.g. alienability) in feudal land-ownership, with the full-scale private ownership of land under capitalism, which reduces land to a mere commodity alongside others and produces legal rules governing its transmission and acquisition parallel to those governing other commodity transactions. To put the same point in legal terms, following Honoré:[36]

> . . . there is a case for saying that, in the early middle ages, land in England could not plausibly be said to be 'owned' because the standard incidents . . . were so divided between lord and tenant that the position of neither presented a sufficient analogy with the paradigm case of owning a thing.

For Hegel, the lack of full-scale land-ownership in nineteenth century Germany was a sign of the irrationality of the legal system (*PR*, §62). For Marx and Engels, it was a sign of its relative backwardness in the process of assimilating capitalist production relations.

(b) It has generated relatively abstract items for ownership which did not exist under previous productive systems. As items enter the commodity market on a large scale (e.g. photographs, films, records), their producers enter into relations with consumers and with owners of capital, and laws have to be produced or adapted to regulate these relations to the benefit of capital.[37] At the other end of the market, the demands of the developing productive system for different kinds of funding produce regulations to protect the interests of owners of capital entering new and ever more complex financial relations.

(3) It has made more generally available secure titles to private property, giving an individual owner security against anyone else with a different title. This is consistent with[38]

> . . . the existence of a power to expropriate or divest in the state or public authorities . . . [provided that] when expropriation takes place, adequate compensation should be paid; but a general right to expropriate, subject to paying compensation, would be fatal to the institution of ownership as we know it.

Under normal circumstances 'the transmission of ownership is consensual'[39] and the right to enforce 'non-consensual' transmission (forcible entry, seizure and disposal) of private property belongs to the agents of the state alone. This again stands in contrast to ownership under feudalism, which distinguished less sharply between agents of public and of private power and failed to provide against forcible 'private expropriation'.

Legal rights

The concept of a legal right was elaborated for the first time by the Roman jurists in their exposition of ownership relations. Jones says that:[40]

> . . . the Greeks never worked out anything resembling the modern notion of a legal right. Though a juridical decision in favour of a party resulted in some benefit to him, something personally or economically advantageous to his interests, it was relative rather than absolute, expressing a preference rather than sanctifying a claim against all and sundry . . . If they had no word for ownership as a right distinct from possession or servitude, it was because they had not pushed the analysis of the notion of a legal right, particularly in its application to material things, as far as later ages have done.

Marx and Engels explained the development of the concept of legal right in Roman law in terms of the development of the commodity market in the Empire.[41] Legal rights developed in direct correlation with the assimilation of more people into the commodity market, but their extension was always limited by the persistence of the class of slaves, unable to 'enter into exchange for the purpose of acquiring anything' and excluded from legal relations (*G*, pp. 245–6). The universalization of legal rights came only with the universalization of commodity production under capitalism.

Contradictions and progress

Capitalism has extended private property further than any previous system in the sense outlined above. It has destroyed the remnants of communal joint ownership which maintained 'natural', organic links between the people and their common possessions, most importantly, the land.[42] In its place it has extended universally Honoré's 'basic model' of a 'single human being, owning in the full liberal sense a single material thing'.[43] But at the same time the development of capitalist relations has made this model increasingly inapplicable. In particular, the development of corporation law for 'the convenience of unifying the common interests of a large number of people and working out as one unit a host of similar individual jural relations',[44] allowing individuals to 'carry on business with limited liability',[45] has tended to deprive most of the corporate owners of the effective exercise of important incidents of ownership, most importantly that of management.[46]

In other words, capitalism has destroyed the old forms of communal property and replaced them by private property as a universal form. It has developed legal categories corresponding to simple commodity exchange. In its development it has generated new forms of joint ownership, forms quite distinct from the old communal ownership, which have also received legal endorsement. They are distinct from any previous forms in that (1) they establish free disposal and acquisition of shares (this corresponds to Honoré's basic model) but also (2) they establish a distance between the owner and the thing owned, which in most cases deprives any particular individual of real control over the property.[47]

Responsibility and Liability

Most jurists would agree that the progress made by modern law towards 'legal individualism' can be measured in part by its success in clarifying and emphasizing the role of the individual agent and of his mental state in assessing culpability. It has made progress on the following four fronts:

(1) It has elaborated the category of *mens rea*.[48]
(2) Within category (1) it has clarified the distinction between intentional and negligent actions.
(3) It has marked off offences involving *mens rea* from offences in which the proof of *mens rea* is not required. It has greatly reduced the scope of this latter category, i.e. the category of offence in which strict liability is applicable.
(4) It has tended to eliminate vicarious liability.

The progress on these four fronts has been to establish that 'as a general rule, no act is sufficient basis of responsibility unless it is done either wilfully or negligently'.[49]

But again, with respect to these categories, we should be wary of over-generalization. For example, Pashukanis regarded the absence of distinctions (2) and (3) as important features of 'archaic criminal law', which[50]

> . . . knew only the concept of harm. Fault and culpability – which occupy so important a place in modern criminal law – were completely absent . . . Premeditated actions, careless action, fortuitous action, were appraised solely by reference to their consequences.

He substantiated this thesis by rather sketchy empirical references, e.g. to the homicide laws of the Ossetians. A similar thesis was maintained by Adkins[51] in relation to the homicide laws described in the Homeric poems. But in the light of work in the anthropology of law, we should be hesitant about asserting such a thesis except in terms of a very general tendency: for Moore has shown quite conclusively that in certain non-modern legal systems motive and intention are weighed as important elements in assessing culpability.[52] Equally, it appears to be impossible to eliminate offences of strict liability altogether from the most advanced systems of civil law regulating business operations.

In the areas of progress listed, the elimination of vicarious liability would seem to be the most essential prerequisite for a fully individualist legal system. It seems self-evident that 'normally and naturally, the person who is responsible for a wrong is he who does it'.[53] But even here we should be wary of too sweeping generalizations, such as this one of Salmond's:[54]

> In more primitive systems . . . the impulse to extend the incidence of liability receives free scope in a manner altogether alien to modern notions of justice.

The reason for our caution is that here, as in other domains, the progress made by modern law is not smooth or direct, since it is determined as much by the requirements of modern business practice as by 'modern notions of justice'; thus the two areas where vicarious liability survives in modern English law are both in civil law: the responsibility of 'masters for the acts of their servants done in the course of their employment' and the liability of the 'representative of dead men . . . for deeds done in the flesh by those whom they represent'.[55] Though juridically anomalous, these survivals are necessitated by the requirements of regulation of business.

Instrumentalism

In so far as Marx and Engels considered the law at the level of immediate political practice, their approach was almost wholly instrumental. In other words they viewed the law as an instrument which might, under certain circumstances be used to further the working class's struggle for particular objectives, even at the expense of what their critics might dub paternalism.[56] The most important issue here was the struggle to establish a legally limited working day, in which Marx aimed for the 'establishment of an all-powerful social barrier which will forbid even the workers themselves from entering into a free contract with capital when by the terms of that contract they and their race are condemned to death or sold into slavery' (*Cap.*, I. pp. 301–2). He described the Factory Acts as a necessary curb on capitalists' 'blind eagerness for plunder' which had 'exhausted the vital energies of the nation' (*Cap.*, I. pp. 238–9). At the same time he saw them as a method of preserving the relatively long-term interests of the capitalist class as a whole from the effect of each capitalist's blind impulse to exploit its labour force to the maximum, an impulse which is unavoidable 'owing to free competition, the immanent laws of capitalist production [which] hold sway irresistibly over every individual capitalist' (ibid., p. 266). This impulse could not be contained unless capitalists were 'forced to pay heed to these matters by social compulsion' (ibid.). But there was no automatic mechanism within the system which operated to enforce these checks on individual capitalists. Their emergence depended on the power of the working class itself which, with increasing organization and discipline, exerted pressure on parliament to endorse the limits of exploitation established in the economic class struggle and to impose the legal backing of the Factory Acts (ibid., p. 283).

So Marx and Engels envisaged these regulations from two aspects: first, they saw them historically as a necessary condition of the temporary survival of the system of capitalist exploitation, since they prevent the exhaustion of the labour force which would otherwise occur (ibid., p. 266); second, they saw them instrumentally as a step on the path towards a complete change in the balance of power in the struggle for control over the means of production. From this dual perspective, capitalist formations, as a condition of their own survival, had to be transformed, both at the level of production relations and at the level of the legal rules embodying and endorsing those relations.

But the view that the instrumental requirement of the class struggle automatically coincides with the functional requirement of a transition from capitalism to socialism depends on an underlying assumption that capitalism is doomed, by virtue of its internal dynamic (underconsumption, falling rate of profit, etc.), to succumb to catastrophic crises. But if that catastrophe theory is false, and there seems reason to think that it is, then the form of both economic and political transformation remains open and it remains always possible that continuing regulations like the Factory Acts could ensure not just the temporary, but the permanent, survival of capitalist relations within a given society.

3.3 THE 'RATIONAL KERNEL' OF MARXIST HISTORICISM

On the withering-away of the superstructures

In an earlier paper[57] I expounded at some length Marx's and Engels's distinction between base and superstructure and their vision of the withering-away of superstructural forms of social relations (political, legal, etc.) with the advent of communism. In that paper I marshalled all the arguments I could muster for the withering-away thesis, but concluded by endorsing only a restricted, hypothetical version of it, whose conclusion I summarize in this section, without, however, recapitulating the lengthy exegesis of the Marxist texts which underpinned the original version.

In bare outline, Marx and Engels theorized as follows:[58] every social formation has an economic structure, consisting of production relations, i.e. relations of productive capacity of sets of individuals *vis-à-vis* means of production and fellow individuals; furthermore, with the exception of primitive communal societies and the predicted communist societies which stand on the horizons of historical study, the capacity relations of every society embody relations of unequal power between different sets of individuals. Power is divided unequally between[59]

> . . . those who exercise control over the means of production, the process of production and its results and those who are deprived of that control although they are the direct producers of the goods . . . These two groups of people form the antagonistic social classes.

In the Marxist picture, all developed societies studied by historians embody relations of unequal power, class relations or relations of exploitation, which allow 'intellectual and material activity – enjoyment and labour, production and consumption – [to] devolve on different individuals' (*CW*, 5, p. 45). In order to maintain a stable system in which power over production and enjoyment of products is thus unequally allocated, a set of further institutions is required. These are the institutions which constitute the superstructure, seen as standing over and above production relations in two senses:

(1) A certain level of surplus productivity must be attained before specialized superstructural agents, not themselves directly productive, can be recruited and maintained: in this sense, superstructural agents, exist over and above productive agents.
(2) The function of the superstructure is to impose a level of unity, cohesion and integration over and above the disunited and indeed antagonistic interests of the members of the classes composing the society.

There are two ways in which this function is performed:

(1) By the direct enforcement of sets of rules which serve the interests of the exploiting class.
(2) By the ideological presentation of particular interests as the general interests of society as a whole.

Marx and Engels envisaged that the superstructure would disappear with the abolition of the class struggle, since, when classes were superseded, the antagonisms associated with them would also be superseded; that the function of the superstructure would then become redundant; that when it became redundant, so too would the division of labour between material producers, on the one hand, and politicians, lawyers, policemen and so on, on the other.

In his classic statement of the envisaged order in the *Anti-Dühring,* Engels referred to the withering-away only of the state, not of all components of the superstructure:

> State interference in social relations becomes, in one domain after another, superfluous, and then withers away of itself, the government of persons is replaced by the administration of things and by the conduct of processes of production. The state is not 'abolished'. It withers away. (*AD,* p. 385)

Was Engels, then, propounding a modest thesis to the effect that the coercive function of the superstructures might disappear under communism, while its other (innocent) features would remain? These would include the existence of a separate level of agents, performing specialized functions, corresponding (in some sense) to the functions presently embodied in the administrative, legal and political systems. The classic formula from the *Civil War in France* suggests such a distinction:

> While the merely repressive organs of the old governmental power were to be amputated, its legitimate functions were to be wrested from an authority usurping preeminence over society itself and restored to the responsible agents of society. (*MESW*, p. 292)

The formula is ambiguous in contrasting 'the *merely* repressive organs' [my emphasis] of class society to the 'legitimate functions' of the transitional order, without explicitly excluding coercion from the latter. The ambiguity of the *Civil War in France,* one of Marx's latest texts, is already present in the *Manifesto* of 1848:

> When in the course of development class distinctions have disappeared and all production has been concentrated in the hands of the associated individuals, then the public power will lose its political character. Political power, properly so called, is merely the organised power of one class for oppressing another. (*MESW*, p. 53)

Here again, the explicit claim is that 'public power' would be transformed under communism, in so far as 'political power', defined functionally as a mode of class oppression, would cease to exist. But the question whether it would be replaced by any coercive apparatus is not posed, let alone answered. The absence of any explicit statement of the modest thesis is due to the incoherence of that thesis. It is incoherent in that it envisages the necessity of maintaining a system of rights and duties (thus negating the utopian convergence-transparency picture of 1843/4, yet does not envisage the necessity of any coercive system to enforce those rights and duties (a tacit return to utopianism). Against it I should maintain that the juridico-political superstructure is in this sense indivisible: rights and duties that are not enforceable are not real rights and duties and, consequently, if rights and duties do play a real role under communism, so too do the coercive agencies which enforce them.

In contrast to that hesitant modest thesis, it is clear that in the early writings, in the *Grundrisse* and, in residual form, in many of the mature texts, Marx and Engels held to the extreme thesis, to the effect that, under communism, all superstructural levels would cease to exist. That thesis, unlike the modest thesis, is coherent, but, as we have seen in the examination of Marx's model of *Gemeinschaftlichkeit*, it depends on a wholly questionable vision of cognitive transparency and harmonization of interests.

But if the extreme version is to be abandoned as utopian metaphysics and the modest version is incoherent, what remains of the withering-away thesis? Only this, I think: any withering-away of the legal superstructures in a classless society would be at most uneven and partial. If the law ceased to perform certain class oppressive functions, its role in enforcing personal civil rights would be enforced. The rational kernel of the base/superstructure distinction and the withering-away thesis can be expressed in three propositions:

(1) Superstructures enforce power relations between individuals and sets of individuals.
(2) Coercive superstructures cannot be 'detached' from the rest, leaving a 'residue' of 'innocent' functions to be performed in a classless society.

(3) Superstructures are a necessary feature of a classless society.

If there could be such a thing as a classless society, it could be envisaged less as a static state than as the 'real movement' of the *German Ideology*:

Communism is for us not a state of affairs which is to be established, an ideal to which reality will have to adjust itself. We call communism the real movement [*wirkliche Bewegung*] which abolishes the present state of things. (*CW*, 5, p. 49. W, 3, pp. 35–6)

Instead of seeing communism as a continent which is reached with the aid of the vehicle of the superstructures, a vehicle which is then abandoned because no longer required, we should see it rather as the locus of conflicting tendencies: a tendency towards the withering-away of the superstructural enforcement of labour discipline, combined with the maintenance of superstructural agencies to enforce personal rights and duties.

A classless society would always be open to the possibility that the class struggle could re-emerge within it, as sets of individuals could monopolize power over decision-making and allocation of resources. A classless society would be a movement, in so far as it would always be faced by sets of decisions which could be potential generators of class conflict. For this reason it would require political and administrative structures to guarantee the rights and enforce the duties of individuals. These structures would be non-class-oppressive but, in so far as the class struggle would always be a possibility, they would embody recognizably superstructural features and their agents would have recognizably superstructural functions. Here we have the germ of an explanation, within Marx's and Engels's theory, of the 'survival' of superstructures under communism.

Base/superstructure and historicism

At the heart of the specifically Marxist contribution to social science lies the base/superstructure model of social organization, summarized above, and a historicist account of social development comprising the following three theses:

(1) The development of the productive forces is a universal force for historical change.
(2) A functional relation holds between forces and relations of production, such that production relations fostering the development of the productive forces flourish, those 'fettering' its development wither and are ultimately 'burst asunder'.
(3) In so far as that functional determination conflicts with intentional agency, the latter is overridden by the former.

Despite the objections of numerous Marxist critics, I accept Marx's own claim that the combination of these two components ((1) the synchronic component, the base/superstructure distinction, and (2) the diachronic component, productive force historicism) 'served as a guiding thread of [his] studies' ('1859 Preface', *MESW*, p. 182). G. A. Cohen's work has shown conclusively both that it is correct to attribute that position to Marx and that it is internally coherent, not flawed by elementary logical errors. Cohen has, however, always been guarded about the substantive question of the truth of 'Karl Marx's theory of history', adducing certain persuasive historical examples, but not wishing to substantiate the parallel between the universal roles of spirit in Hegel and of the productive forces in Marx:[60]

> For Hegel . . . history shows an expansion of consciousness giving itself form in cultures, which subvert themselves through their success in advancing consciousness . . . For Marx . . . the important forms are not cultures but economic structures, and the role of consciousness is assumed by expanding productive power.

I should, myself, be even more wary than Cohen of generalizing the historicist model of irresistible productive forces breaking through the fetters of inhibiting production relations which is inapplicable to certain great historical transformations, in particular to the 'Decline and Fall of the Roman Empire'.[61]

We can, in fact, distinguish quite sharply between the two components of historical materialism, the synchronic and the diachronic. According to the synchronic component, a given type of economic structure (feudal, capitalist, etc.) is compatible with only a limited range of superstructural forms (legal, political, etc.) and operates both 'by blocking or selecting out all such phenomena which do not comply with it' and by mapping 'the actual content' of the superstructures.[62] This component is acceptable, within closely defined limits. Most plausibly, it can be taken as describing a relation between economic relations, on the one hand, and superstructural relations on the other. Combining this synchronic component with a modest version of the diachronic component, we can say that in capitalist formations all juridical modes of categorizing individuals embodying degrees of personal dependence give way to the dominant category of free subject of rights, which is the only category capable of expressing at the legal level the operations of a free market in labour power, the central element of the capitalist mode of production. It is important to stress the modesty of this position. First, I reject any functionalism according to which a particular superstructure is present in a given society only in so far as it successfully fulfills the function of reproducing the production relations of that society. The range of functions performed by an advanced legal system transcends and can outlast the capitalist relations it was called forth to endorse. How far it will do that is to some extent an open question, and this is because thesis (3) of historicism is itself of only limited applications. As Lichtheim put it:[63]

> The principle that social being determines consciousness must be understood as itself an historical one: it refers to a state of affairs which has characterised history from the very beginning, but which is due to disappear when a rational order has been created. For the attainment of such an order implies the conscious direction of social life, hence the emancipation of consciousness from blind, uncomprehended necessity.

We can now see why reductionist functionalism combined with universal historicism, including thesis (3), makes Marxism so inimical to posing substantive questions of jurisprudence from the 'internal point of view'. The three available perspectives are (1) the wholly negative one of the contrast between the given legal order and the envisaged *Gemeinschaft* lying beyond, (2) the more positive one of unfolding legal rationality and (3) the neutral one of pure instrumentalism. All three remain external to endorsement of or first-person participation in the legal-constitutional process and equally external to the elaboration of the meta-categories of jurisprudence, in so far as that discipline is continuous with the practice of the law itself. As Unger has rightly observed, in jurisprudence, as in the other 'dogmatic' disciplines, grammar, theology and (he might have added) philosophy, there is no[64]

> . . . clear distinction between the object accounted for and the account itself. On the one hand, the grammar, the theology, or the legal doctrine participates in the evolution of the language, the religion, or the law, helping define its shape and determine its directions. On the other hand, the categories of the grammarian, the doctrines of the theologian, or the reasonings of lawyers and judges are drawn from the very tradition they expound and develop. Lastly, because of the intimate relationship between the account and its object, every claim in a dogmatic discipline is an elaboration of some point of view already present in the community with which the discipline is associated.

The strength of the Marxist ideology critique lay in its rigorous and brutal externality to the practice or institution of which it was the critique. But this was also its weakness, in so far as the internal point of view, expressed in lived relations, forms of participation etc., distanced itself from the externalist model demanded by Marxist critical reductionism.

In Marx's and Engels's texts positive endorsement of legal values from the internal point of view is rare indeed. Here is one of the few examples:

> Let us not forget that if English law continues to express the economic relations of capitalistic society in that barbarous feudal language which corresponds to the thing expressed . . . that same English law is the only one which has preserved through ages, and transmitted to America and the Colonies, the best part of that old Germanic personal freedom, local self-government and independence from all interference but that of the law courts which on the Continent has been lost during the period of absolute monarchy, and

has nowhere been as yet fully recovered. (F. Engels, *Socialism, Utopian and Scientific*, special introduction to the English edition of 1892, *MESW*, pp. 391–2)

After attributing a definite historical origin to the value of 'personal freedom, local self-government and freedom from all interference but that of the law courts', Engels did not thereby devalue it or envisage it as a mere historical relic. Rather he endorsed a historical, cultural tradition, without directly founding that endorsement in either functionalist-progressive or immediate instrumental terms. But that text by Engels remained isolated in the dominant functionalism/instrumentalism of Marxist jurisprudence.

We might conjecture that Marx presupposed a hidden hand working through the development of the productive forces, to make the legal system more rational both in rationally expressing the production relations, themselves functionally tied to the productive forces, and in universalizing the values of the *Rechtsstaat*, the world of embodied personal liberties. But the best that can be said for that conjecture is that the hidden hand brings the poles together only in the most haphazard manner: in some conjunctures, the struggles for constitutional rights and civil liberties may coincide with a move towards economic rationalization, but by no means always.

Given these reservations, a rational kernel, a critical perspective for viewing utopian jurisprudence, including Marx's own flirtations with *Gemeinschaftlichkeit*, can be extracted from historical materialism, which is that there are material constraints upon the range of superstructures compatible with a given technological development. Thus the maintenance of advanced technology, in particular of high information technology is not compatible with a reversion to simple, face-to-face, transparent relations between individuals. It is compatible with a number of other superstructural forms, ranging from a quasi-monopoly control over centralized means of information by a ruling group to a constitutionally defended system of access to given information and control over the use made of it, available to citizens in individual and corporate capacities. How far a given society corresponds to one or other extreme of this spectrum can be gauged by reference to two criteria: the formal criterion of the presence or absence of constitutional rights and their specification in particular statutes; and the concrete criterion of the availability of means of enforcing these rights in practice.

Marxist and Hegelian historicism

Erinnerung *and negation of the negation*

I should also want to isolate the rational kernel of Marx's historicism from a central element of the Hegelian dialectic, namely the idealist notion of the negation of the negation.

For Hegel, the spiritual subject exercises its rationality by internalizing whatever is presented to it, by annulling the independence of the external and making it an expression or sphere of itself. Spirit performs this internalization in all its activities: artistic creation, religious experience, scientific knowledge and philosophy.

But at the same time, in so far as the subject has to find itself in objects, i.e. to externalize itself or objectify itself, its object has to remain brute, unstructured, impenetrable by reason. There has to remain a real objectivity over and against subjectivity, not fully permeated by subjective rationality; otherwise the subject will not after all be able to find another in which to recognize itself. The need for a brute, contingent realm is an important theme of Hegel's natural philosophy and of his political philosophy. At any point of dialectical development, and thus at each level of reality, the subject generates an irreducible level of brute objectivity in order to exist.

Against this, it must be recognized that since the dialectic is a movement or process, and because objectification and expression are the motors of this process, no state of objectivity can be considered absolute or final *vis-à-vis* the subject.

The motor of the Hegelian dialectic is the essential tension between the two aspects of Spirit's activity, expression and objectification. That tension can be resolved in the restoration (or 'recollection') of a state of unity, as the object, the negation of the subject, is itself negated. In this negation of the negation, what was already present, implicitly, in the subject is brought out in a resolution that was already contained in the origin of the subject.

The Hegelian notion of the negation of the negation, the uncovering of features of a system already implicitly contained within it in the dialectical *Erinnerung* (recollection-internalization) is one that surfaces repeatedly in historicist versions of Marxism. The suggestion is that in the negation of a one-sided, abstract feature of the present order (e.g. 'bourgeois freedom'), the real, concrete content of that feature can be brought out. But this whole vocabulary of 'negation' and 'bringing-out' can be dangerously ambivalent. As Hegel himself clearly recognized and welcomed in his idealist system, it puts in question the criterion of identity of the object or property which is the subject of the developing process. But whether it can properly be transposed into the materialist key is, as we have already seen, questionable.

Marx himself, from the early *Manuscripts* to the mature texts of *Capital*,[65] was constantly tempted by this Hegelian notion:

> . . . this so-called *Original Accumulation* means nothing but a series of historical processes, resulting in a Decomposition of the *Original Union* existing between the Labouring Man and his Instruments of Labour. The *Separation* between the Man of Labour and the Instruments of Labour once established, such a state of things will maintain itself and reproduce itself upon a constantly increasing scale, until a new and fundamental revolution in the mode of production should again overturn it, and restore the original union in a new historical form. (*Wage, Labour and Capital*, *MESW*, p. 210)

'Original Union', 'fundamental revolution', 'restore the original union': all the components of the Hegelian dialectic are there, never fully to be exorcized from Marxism.

A far more modest thesis can, I think be extracted from Marx's and Engels's writings, shorn of the metaphysics both of the dialectical recall (*Erinnerung*) of the *Aufhebung* and of the spurious necessity of the emergence of the new form from the womb of the old. According to that modest thesis, history is a process in which social formations embodying particular economic structures generate, in virtue of those structures, contradictions or relations of incompatibility between their productive powers and their production relations. As Engels summarized:

> Marx merely shows from history that just as formerly petty industry by its very development created the conditions of its own annihilation . . . so now the capitalist mode of production has likewise itself created the material conditions from which it must perish. (*AD*, pp. 182 ff.)

The thesis is that, in reproducing its relations over time, a capitalist formation is forced to destroy those same relations: and the same is claimed to be true of formations embodying other exploitative production relations. At the same time, a capitalist formation which generates such a contradiction also generates the conditions or materials for transforming its relations into ones which are adequate to contain its productive forces. There is no suggestion that the transformation of the old relations into new ones is merely a process of laying bare implicit features of the old ones or that the resolution of the contradiction was already contained in the old system. Rather, the old system, itself the outcome of practices put through sets of relations, provides the conditions under which agents' practices can effectively be brought to bear on existing relations to transform them. Shorn of the Hegelian metaphysical rhetoric, Marxist historicism, like Sampson, loses much of its grandeur and strength: such is the fate of giants of former times.

Hegelian dialectic and philosophical anthropology: G. A. Cohen

In his paper 'Marx's dialectic of labor', Cohen aimed to extract a 'descriptive' (though not necessarily explanatory) picture of the dialectic from Hegel:[66]

> In seeing a dialectic in a process we discern a contour in an intellectually satisfying manner, but the explanation why it unfolds as it does is not thereby disclosed to us. I am not asserting that there is something necessarily natural about a dialectical sequence . . . But I do think that many processes in which subject and object are implicated in a changing relation are well conceived as transition from undifferentiated unity through differentiated disunity to differentiated unity . . . This conclusion of the dialectic is the descriptive residue of a conclusion which Hegel certainly and Marx perhaps thought had explanatory import as well. Whether it admits of explanatory construal is a question not pursued here. (p. 237)

But Cohen found it hard (not surprisingly for a philosopher) to stick to this austerely descriptive programme. It turns out that he was not simply elaborating an intellectually satisfying pattern for the depiction of historical sequences, with no explanatory purchase. In fact he offered quite a complex explanatory schema involving productive forces, production relations and 'experiences' ('phenomenologies'), the latter corresponding to the 'ideological forms' of the '1859 Preface':

> (1) The respective experiences of craftsman and proletarian, the contrasting phenomenologies of their everyday lives reflect and consolidate similarly antithetical ownership positions. (p. 244)
>
> (2) . . . craft production keeps men attached to nature by blocking the further development of the productive faculty it once advanced, since it hinders the collectivization of labour which is a premise of increasing productivity. (p. 245)

The second formulation (2) is a straightforward application of the 'Preface' thesis that moments of historical contradiction or crisis are moments when production relations which previously fostered the development of the productive forces now obstruct or fetter that development. Cohen's original contribution is the first formulation, (1), which explicates Marx's 'additional answer on the level of philosophical anthropology' (additional to his 'economic' answer) 'to the question why capitalist, and not pre-capitalist, arrangements are capable of sponsoring great advances in production' (p. 251).

But the 'philosophical anthropology' of historical progress is problematic with respect to its units of analysis. Cohen had begun his account with a presentation of Hegel's dialectic of love, the passage of a relationship through three phases: combined lives with identical interests/hostility to a continued connection/a new harmony consisting of the non-antagonistic individuality of the two partners. Here the bearers of the dialectic are particular human beings, whose experiences can be mapped over time (pp. 236–7). In contrast, in the 'philosophical anthropology' of the historical dialectic, it is less clear what the bearers of the process are. It is, of course, the charm of Hegel's historical dialectics, particularly in the *Phenomenology*, that Spirit, the bearer of the process, is always, necessarily, unseen, 'behind' (and increasingly 'in') its manifestations, and the tremendous historical leaps that Hegel makes are justified by reference to Spirit's unseen presence. After the epistemological dialectics of the opening of the *Phenomenology,* it is not necessarily the same individual or even the same people or historical epoch that undergoes a given dialectical transformation. For a materialist, however, the hidden hand of Spirit is not available and if the anthropological dialectic is to have any purchase, it must be possible to attach it to some subject or bearer: but which? How can the anthropological sequence be made more concrete and specific? Cohen's thesis would appear to be a two part one: the second part stating that feudalism is a necessary precondition for capitalism and capitalism is a necessary precondition for socialism; the first part stating that the 'experience of the craftsman' is a necessary precondition for the 'experience of the proletarian' and the 'experience of the proletarian' is a necessary precondition for the 'experience of the socialist'. If that is the correct reading, then the problem of attaching experiences to subjects becomes acute. It is not clear whether particular individuals, classes or generations are envisaged as the bearers.

If we compare Cohen's *Bildungsroman* with a rather more concrete account of historical evolution in Western Europe, that of Henri Pirenne, the two pictures look markedly different. For Cohen, the movement from feudalism to capitalism takes the form of a movement from 'engulfing' labour, in which the labourer is 'merged' with his task, to 'fragmented' labour, in which he is distanced from, and indifferent to, both his work and its products. For Pirenne, the craft guild, at least in its developed form in late feudalism, can be understood as 'an industrial corporation enjoying the monopoly of practising a particular profession, in accordance with regulation sanctioned by public authority'.[67] A master craftsman is an independent entrepreneur, his capital consisting of his house and necessary tools, number of employees limited by regulation, immune (by regulation again) from competition. The technical process (whether a whole artefact or part of an artefact was produced in the workshop) was determined by the place of the city in international trade. For Pirenne, in other words, the work process with the craft guild could take very many different forms (some corresponding to Cohen's model of 'merged' labour, others wholly opposed to it), while the guild itself performed a range of economic functions within the feudal productive system.

Now Cohen was too subtle a thinker to ignore the variety of forms of division labour possible under feudalism: 'Precapitalist weavers and tanners participated in several stages of the respective production processes, and weaving operations differed significantly in kind from tanning operations, and among themselves' (p. 247). Yet, Cohen maintained, following Marx, there was a qualitative difference between feudalism's still relatively specialized artisanal skills and 'capitalism's ideal [which] is to homogenize tasks across and within all branches of production, so that workers may move from job to job doing much the same simple thing in a variety of settings'. The question is therefore not whether, in retrospect, we can distinguish different general forms of the division of labour, broadly characteristic of different modes of production, but rather, given the variety of different forms of production and labour characteristic of late feudalism, what significance the philosophical anthropology of experience of life styles has in understanding the process of transition. Until we know how to distinguish the bearers of significant experiences, the reference to those experiences will be hard to interpret.

At the heart of the Hegelian dialectic is the theme of *Erinnerung*, the remembering/internalizing/recovering of something that was already there implicitly at the start of the process. Cohen's love story is true to that model. The happy couple maintain their own (transformed) identity through the dialectical process in relation to a continuing (transformed) object, their love. Both subject and object of the process can be identified over time in a relatively straightforward way. We have already seen that the identification of the subject in the dialectic of historical anthropology is not so easy. The same is true of the object: just what is maintained/transformed in the historical process?

Craft labor *can* be unengulfing, but if engulfed craft labor is the point of departure, transition to craft labor without engulfment requires the demise of craft labor and the rise of proletarian.

The identity of the process is maintained by the identity of the object, labour: engulfing craft labour/alienating proletarian labour/craft labour free of its original 'idiocy'. The identity of the object is asserted unequivocally: it 'reappears':

> Proletarian labor effects a break with the engulfment craft labor promoted, but it thereby enables craft labor to reappear free of its original 'idiocy'. Similarly, a meaningful work process which is also enslaving cannot just lose its enslaving quality but can appear without it after a phase during which the work process lacks meaning. (p. 256)

As always, Cohen avoided any simple traps. He was not directly attributing advocacy of a dialectically transformed form of craft labour to Marx, merely showing 'that such favor would be compatible with his doctrine of the engulfment inherent in historical craft labor' (ibid.). My difference with Cohen does not concern exegesis: his nuanced reading of the *Grundrisse* is precise. Rather it concerns the plausibility of the anthropological sketch itself. Just what 'experience of labour' is it suggested that the subjects of the historical dialectic must pass through? Even if certain individuals (classes, generations) can be identified who have made the passage through these experiences, would it be true to say that the new form of labour was a transformed form of the old? What, in the tiresome phrase of the old analytical philosophy, would be the criteria of identity of the form?

In summary, my reservations concern:

(1) The possibility of modelling historical developments (transformations of social structures) on biographical developments (phenomenologies of personal experience).
(2) The possibility of specifying both the subjects and the objects of the historical phenomenology.
(3) The possibility of extracting a non-metaphysical, materialist analog of the Hegelian *Erinnerung*, without which

> the moments of the dialectical process lose their inner connection.

My own, more sceptical, view, already sketched above, is that the Gordian knot of the Hegel–Marx connection should be quite brutally cut. New forms should be seen not as dialectically transformed forms of old ones and their authenticity cannot therefore be verified by means of dialectical recall. My more brutal position is that new forms are bought only at a price. The price of the *Gesellschaft* is precisely the loss of the security, intimacy, immediacy that constitutes the *Gemeinschaft*. The dialectical approach suggests that, in the best of all possible worlds, no such price has to be paid, since everything that is lost is regained, in a new and better form. The argument developed so far suggests that that is the essence of the metaphysic of nostalgia.

NOTES

1. A lucid account of the ambivalences of Marx and his successors on this subject is to be found in S. Lukes, 'Marxism, morality and justice', 1982.
2. The exploration of the *gemeinschaftlich* element in Marx's work was launched (or re-launched) in the English literature by G. A. Cohen ('Marx's dialectic of labor', 1974), who related it back to its Hegelian dialectical source. It has been subsequently developed by R. Keat, who has located it in relation to Tönnies's *Gemeinschaft/Gesellschaft* distinction.
3. As heralded in Locke's *Letter on Toleration*.
4. For abbreviations used to refer to Marx's and Engel's texts, see Bibliography.
5. L. Kolakowski, 'The myth of human self-identity', 1977.
6. R. Keat, 'Individualism and community in socialist thought', 1981 (abbreviated to ICST); 'Liberal rights and socialism', 1982 (abbreviated to LRS). Page references to Keat in the text of this section are to these two papers.
7. For a discussion of Kamenka's and Tay's model of 'bureaucratic-administrative regulation', see section 4.3 below.
8. I return to this central insight of Ronald Dworkin at many points in my reflections.

9. A theme developed with precision by Max Weber, *Economy and Society*, 1968 edition, p. 729.
10. R. Unger, *Law in Modern Society*, p. 193.
11. J. Michael, *The Politics of Secrecy*, 1982, p. 124, p. 125.
12. See the *Guardian*, 11 December 1982, 10 January 1983, for Tory resistance to enforcement of Art. 119.
13. J. C. Adams and P. Barile, *The Government of Republican Italy*, 1972, p. 55.
14. P. Stein and P. Shand, *Legal Values in Western Society*, 1974, p. 129.
15. G. Heiman, 'The sources and significance of Hegel's corporate doctrine', 1971, pp. 113 ff. shows that this judgement of the historical school of law is not entirely fair. He also shows that Hegel's own position between legal 'historicism' and 'rationalism' is not unequivocal.
16. Quoted by S. Hook, *From Hegel to Marx: Studies in the Intellectual Development of Karl Marx*, 1968, p. 141. His account of 'Marx on the historical school' (pp. 141–4) is interesting.
17. *Ludwig Feuerbach and the End of Classical German Philosophy, MESW*, p. 627; Introduction to the English edition of *Socialism, Utopian and Scientific, MESW*, pp. 391–2.
18. *Origin of the Family, Private Property and the State, MESW.*, pp. 509–10.
19. *G*, pp. 245–6; *AD*, pp. 142–3.
20. *G*, pp. 163–5, Gmn. p. 81–2.
21. *G*, p. 243, Gmn. p. 154. Though, as we have seen in section 3.1, Marx's endorsement of these progressive features of the *Rechtsstaat* was modified throughout the *Grundrisse* by his nostalgic hankerings for the lost *Gemeinschaft*.
22. S.F. Moore, 'Legal liability and evolutionary interpretation: some aspects of strict liability, self-help and collective responsibility', 1972, p. 56.
23. Sir Henry Maine, *Ancient Law*, 1965 edition, p. 74.
24. Ibid., p. 100.
25. *Origin of the Family, Private Property and the State, MESW*, p. 514.
26. The unevenness of the transition from feudalism to capitalism in different societies should not be under-emphasized. In England the process was constantly obstructed by Tudor governments, which attempted to block the emergence of capitalist relations by reimposing guild regulations, attempts which foundered on the weakness of central political power and the effective penetration of the judiciary at the JP level by the rising class of gentlemen and merchants. (See Engels, *AD*, pp. 145–6 and C.

Hill, *Reformation to Industrial Revolution,* p. 95.) Elsewhere the balance of forces in the class struggle was different, and the sixteenth century French nobility reacted to the encroachment on their power by the crown and the bourgeoisie by developing the doctrine of *dérogeance,* which was in time endorsed by law, and which prevented the nobility from engaging in trade on pain of losing their privileges; its effect was 'the immobilisation of capital in land'. (H.G. Koenigsberger and G.L. Mosse, *Europe in the XVI Century,* 1971, pp. 40–1).
27. M. Weber, *Economy and Society,* p. 672.
28. A.M. Honoré, 'Ownership'.
29. Ibid.
30. Ibid., p. 109.
31. The 11 incidents are: (1) the right to possess, (2) the right to use, (3) the right to manage, (4) the right to income, (5) the right to capital, (6) the right to security, (7) the incident of transmissibility, (8) the incident of absence of term, (9) prohibition of harmful use, (10) liability to execution, (11) residuary character. (A.M. Honoré, 'Ownership', pp. 111–127).
32. Ibid., p. 114.
33. Ibid., p. 123.
34. D. Lloyd, *The Idea of Law,* p. 324.
35. A.M. Honoré, 'Ownership', p. 123.
36. Ibid., p. 109.
37. Cf. M. Edelman, *The Ownership of the Image.*
38. A.M. Honoré, 'Ownership', pp. 119 ff.
39. Ibid.
40. J.W. Jones, *The Law and Legal Theory of the Greeks,* 1956, p. 151, p. 298.
41. *Ludwig Feuerbach, MESW,* p. 627.
42. See *Grundrisse,* p. 497. For the brutal application of this principle, see A. Soboul, *The French Revolution 1787–1799,* 1974 edition, pp. 188–9.
43. A.M. Honoré, 'Ownership', p. 147.
44. J.W. Salmond, *Jurisprudence,* 1960 edition and J.W.M. Dias, *Jurisprudence,* 1970, chapter 11.
45. J.W. Salmond, *Jurisprudence,* p. 313.
46. 'The great technicality of modern commercial enterprise requires management by experts, a task which the majority of shareholders are utterly incapable of discharging. This has brought about a cleavage between membership and management, for the corporation, being a figure of straw, is incapable of exercising it, nor can the members who usually lack technical knowledge and, in any case, are too large and diffuse a body to

be co-ordinated effectively. It is thus perfectly true . . . that shareholders are now merely the recipients of dividends'. (J.W.M. Dias, *Jurisprudence*, p. 313).

47. In some speculative passages of *Capital* III, Marx envisaged forms of joint ownership endorsed by capitalist law (though restricted to a relatively small class) as 'paving the way' to real joint ownership by the whole of society, on the basis of the higher level of productivity inaugurated by capitalism, joint stock companies representing the 'abolition of the capitalist mode of production within the capitalist mode of production itself', see *Cap.*, III, p. 438. Marx seems to have underestimated capitalism's capacity to survive and adapt.
48. Though it has by no means solved the conceptual problems raised by the application of that category: see H.L.A. Hart, 'Negligence, *Mens Rea* and criminal responsibility', 1961.
49. J.W. Salmond, *Jurisprudence*, p. 375.
50. E.B. Pashukanis, *General Theory of Law and Marxism*, 1951 edition, p. 216.
51. A.W.H. Adkins, *Merit and Responsibility*, 1960, p. 53.
52. See S. F. Moore, 'Legal liability and evolutionary interpretation'.
53. J.W. Salmond, *Jurisprudence*, p. 400.
54. Ibid. For vicarious liability in the Babylonian Code of Hammurabji, see D. Lloyd, *The Idea of Law*, p. 348.
55. J.W. Salmond, *Jurisprudence*, chapter 12.
56. For a clear demonstration that such legislation is not properly described as paternalist, see G. Dworkin, 'Paternalism', 1971, pp. 112–13.
57. T. O'Hagan, 'On the "withering-away" of the superstructures', 1981.
58. Basic works on this topic are G.A. Cohen, 'On some criticisms of historical materialism', 1970, and *Karl Marx's Theory of History: a Defence*, 1978. On Marx's theory of social classes, see W. Wesolowski, 'Marx's theory of class domination', 1967.
59. W. Wesolowski, 'Marx's theory of class domination', pp. 57–8.
60. G.A. Cohen, *Karl Marx's Theory of History*, 1978, p. 26.
61. See the far more plausible account, from a Marxist theoretical standpoint, by G.E.M. de Ste-Croix, *The Class Struggle in the Ancient Green World*, 1981, part 8.
62. J. McMurtry, 'Making sense of economic determinism', 1973, p. 256, p. 258.
63. G. Lichtheim, 'The Concept of Ideology', 1965, pp. 176–7.
64. R.M. Unger, *Knowledge and Politics*, pp. 111–12.

65. The most famous Hegelian echoes in *Capital* are in vol. I, chapter 32, 'The Historical Tendency of Capitalist Accumulation'.
66. Page references in the text in this section are to G.A. Cohen, 'Marx's dialectic of labor'.
67. H. Pirenne, *Economic and Social History of Medieval Europe*, 1937, p. 182.

4

Tönnies and After

4.1 TÖNNIES AND THE FORMALIZATION OF THE *GEMEINSCHAFT/GESELLSCHAFT* DISTINCTION

While the distinction between *Gemeinschaft* and *Gesellschaft* was already present in shadowy form in Hegel and Marx, it was only later sharpened into an explanatory category and applied specifically to jurisprudence by Ferdinand Tönnies, both in his classic *Gemeinschaft und Gesellschaft* (1887)[1] and in his *Einführung in die Soziologie* (1931).[2] Here is Tönnies's introduction to the distinction taken from his autobiographical comment 'My relation to Sociology' (1932):[3]

> As far as the concepts of *Gemeinschaft* and *Gesellschaft* are concerned, it ought to be understood that I don't apply them to the development of a culture in such a way . . . that the former, as a period of youth, is described as 'good', the latter, as a period of senescence, as 'bad', with the consequence that what is good in youth is seen as derived from *Gemeinschaft* while the evil quality of senescence is derived from *Gesellschaft*. . . . My own opinion is very different. I do not know of any condition of culture or society in which elements of *Gemeinschaft* and elements of *Gesellschaft* are not simultaneously present, that is, mixed. Moreover, although *Gemeinschaft*, too, arrives at higher and nobler forms of human relations, it is correct to say that *Gesellschaft* is the essentially variable element which enhances culture but also transforms it into civilization.

Following Tönnies's admonition to use the distinction analytically rather than normatively, we can extract from his work the table of oppositions shown in table 4.1.

Table 4.1. Gemeinschaft/Gesellschaft *Table of Oppositions.*

Gemeinschaft	*Gesellschaft*
(1) Consists of relations between united natural wills, yielding a social self similar in kind to its components.	(1) Consists of relations between arbitrary wills, yielding a superimposed, artificial person.
(2) Its forces are derived from within.	(2) Its forces are derived from without.
(3) Its goals are universal.	(3) Its goals are restricted, particular.
(4) In it, rights and duties condense on each individual.	(4) In it, rights and duties are strictly separate.
(5) In it, there are rights and duties of participation.	(5) In it, there are no rights and duties of participation.
(6) Its law is derived from a union of (1), human beings related as members of a whole.	(6) Its law is derived from free, independent individuals. It upholds the particular rights and duties of those constituents.
(7) Its principle of distribution: to each what has been assigned to him by law and equity.	(7) Its principle of distribution: to each what he has gained, unless conclusively proved that it was earned dishonestly.
(8) Relation between law and morality: merger, in which law submits to morality. Law designed to be an instrument of moral education.	(8) Relation between law and morality: strict separation. Law designed to be useful, not moral.
(9) The goal of life: good living-together, with good will and the desire to provide mutual aid.	(9) The goal of life: peaceful living together, without force.

In this table of oppositions, types of social organization are marked off in terms of their most general features: individualism vs. communalism as principles of recognition of one's place in society; authority vs. competition as principles of distribution; morality vs. utility as goals of social life. At this very general level, it should be noted that the simplicity of the either/or dichotomies is blurred when the oppositions are applied concretely. In the case of law and morality, for instance, the simple dichotomy is between two functions of law: morality vs. utility. But, as table 4.1 shows, the real opposition is between a form in which law and morality are not rigorously separated and one in which they are. Thus the very distinction between utility and morality emerges only in the latter form.

The table of oppositions applies also to the forms in which *Gemeinschaft* and *Gesellschaft* are expressed in legal terms: the emergence in the latter of artificial legal persons and the Hohfeldian schema of rights and duties.

In addition to *Gemeinschaft* vs. *Gesellschaft*, Tönnies introduced a further opposition: union (*Verbindung*), defined as a closed unity (*geschlossene Einheit*), vs. association (*Bündnisverhältnis*), defined as a loose relationship (*löses Verhältnis*).[4] Since both union and association can have either a *gemeinschaftlich* or a *gesellschaftlich* form, four possibilities are available. We find them discussed by Tönnies in the order displayed in figure 4.1.

Tönnies used this four-term schema both diachronically, to illustrate certain historical transitions, and synchronically, to display the possibility of the coexistence of elements within a given society at a given time. Historically, Tönnies saw (2) developing out of (1) in the feudal institutions of guild and church, structured by authority and status, but transcending kinship and geography, allowing for a new level of flexibility, development and movement. Synchronically, Tönnies identified relations of friendship in his own society as falling under (2), with marriage uneasily located between (1) and (2), part *Zusammenwohnen*, part contract. The most obvious combinations are (1) and (3): on the one hand, the world that is communitarian and closed, the world of kinship; on the other, the world that is individualistic and open, the world of the

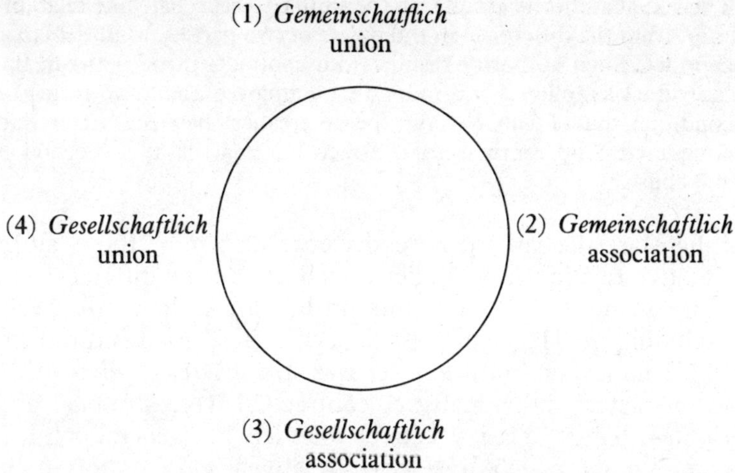

Figure 4.1. Gemeinschaft/Gesellschaft, *Union/Association. Four Possible Combinations.*

capitalist corporation. But for our purposes, the most interesting form is (4), the *gesellschaftlich* union, which 'provides for a union of . . . all with others':[5]

> The union becomes more similar to the Gemeinschaft and the determining arbitrary will more similar to the natural will. The union becomes more general in its extent and its purpose.

This idea allows us to envisage certain features of the social *Rechtsstaat*. It represents a break from the now untenable naturalism of blood and soil and also from the authoritarianism characteristic of many *gemeinschaftlich* institutions.[6] It would replace them with the 'artificial' principles of legal citizenship, rights and duties. But it would also allow the social content of the *Rechtsstaat* to be made real by government intervention in areas abandoned by formalist jurisprudence and *laissez-faire* economics to the arbitrary play of the market.

Tönnies, like Marx and Weber,[7] stressed the hollowness of the juridical equality between the participants in the capitalist labour contract:[8]

The actual authority results, in the simple Gesellschaft-like relationship, from the difference in the power of two parties, as in the labor contract. Such authority results from contracts made between the individual 'employer' and individual 'employee', and also from the condition out of which come 'peace treaties' between victor and conquered. Apparently it is a contract, but in actuality it is coercion and abuse.

Like Marx, he saw the necessity of transforming those 'authoritative relationships' under socialism. But he differed from Marx in marking four points on his circle, thus effectively excluding the Hegelian schema of dialectical triad and return. For Tönnies, any future order was still strictly *gesellschaftlich* in character: individualistic, contractual, constitutional and rights-oriented. Yet it was to be founded on a general political commitment which was to be relatively closed, not to be subverted by external, instrumental considerations: hence a 'union' in Tönniesian terms.

There is no normative advocacy of one form over another, nor any historicist vision of the inevitable transcendence of the given *Gesellschaft* in a new *Gemeinschaft*. Apart from a ritual reference to Hegel and the Hegelian terminology of thesis, antithesis and synthesis in the *Einführung in die Soziologie*, Tönnies's distance from Hegel and from the Hegelian residue in Marx is striking: a vision not of ultimate transcendence of oppositions, but of their conflictual coexistence in all advanced societies.

4.2 PASHUKANIS: LAW AS AN EXPRESSION OF EXCHANGE RELATIONS

Interest in Pashukanis's 'commodity exchange theory' of law has been revived in recent years. Pashukanis has been described as 'the only man who has made a real contribution towards a materialist philosophy of law',[9] as 'the paramount figure in the second attempt [Lenin's *State and Revolution* being the first] to fulfill the Marxist vision of a world without legal coercion'.[10] In his *General Theory of Law and Marxism*, Pashukanis undertook a detailed working out of the connection, sketched by Marx in the *Grundrisse*, between the economic domain of commodity exchange, on the one hand, and the juridical domain of legal subjects, on the other. Pashukanis set himself the question, 'Where shall we search for the unique social relationship whose inevitable reflection is the form of law?' and answered that it is[11]

> Only as freedom of disposition that property becomes the basis of the development of the legal form and the category 'subject' serves as the best expression of that freedom. (p. 160)

> The category 'subject of rights' is an abstraction from acts of exchange in the market. The market association discloses the antithesis of subject and object in the special legal sense. (p. 166)

'Expression' . . . 'abstraction' . . . 'disclosure': these are the terms in which Pashukanis theorized the relationship between the market and the law. Familiar objections have been brought, from within the Marxist camp, to this schema: that it improperly prioritizes exchange over production, that it plays down the coercive role of the state, etc. But these do not concern us here.

It is interesting to note how closely Pashukanis followed the *Gesellschaft* tradition in identifying the legal with the private, promoting the transactions and relations of private law to the paradigm of the legal order as a whole.[12] This involved him in a number of theoretical contortions, in particular in attempting to fit the sanctions of the criminal law to this model.

But for our purposes, the most striking feature of Pashukanis's approach is his use of the vocabulary of 'expression' to designate the relation between the two domains and the explicit counter-model of the social order envisaged after the withering-away of the present one. For Pashukanis, as for Marx of the *Grundrisse*, legal forms, as the 'expressions' of doomed economic relations, are themselves doomed to speedy extinction with the withering-away of the commodity market, in particular the labour market. What distinguishes Pashukanis's approach, apart from its historical and jurisprudential detail, is its explicit espousal of the counter-model of 'technical regulation':

. . . unity of purpose is a premise of technical regulation. Accordingly, the juridic norms of the responsibility of railways presuppose private claims and private isolated interests; whereas the technical rules of railway movement presuppose a single purpose – the attainment of maximum hauling capacity, let us say. The treatment of a sick person – to take another example – presupposes a series of rules, both for the patient himself and for the medical personnel; but inasmuch as these rules are established from the point of view of a single purpose – the restoration of the patient's health – they are of a technical character. In conjunction with their application, there may be a certain constraint as regards the patient. But so long as this constraint is regarded from the view-point of the same purpose (which is identical for the person exerting the constraint and for the person subjected thereto), it remains a measure which is technically expedient – and nothing more. Within these limits, the content of the rules is established by medical science and changes as that science progresses. (pp. 137–8)

According to the model of 'technical regulation', a 'single purpose' would replace the multiplicity of necessarily conflicting purposes in the market. But, as Pashukanis's perceptive critic Schlesinger has pointed out, this[13]

. . . assertion is acceptable if it implies no more than an interpretation of the vast majority of cases of compulsion necessary in the capitalist and also in the transitional society as the consequence of present or recent class divisions. It may be expected that the abolition of such divisions would be followed by a market reduction of the number of cases in which compulsion would be applied.

But, Schlesinger noted, if our model of 'technical regulation' is something like a railway by-law (the example used by Pashukanis), even such a by-law is

. . . always a command addressed to *men* (for the rails and engines, unhappily, do not understand either English or Russian). Whether it works as a mere technical advice which the engine-driver . . . follows because he is convinced of its reasonableness, depends on the general character of the society in the framework of which this railway is run.

In the absence of class exploitation, in other words, social goals might be expected to be not homogeneous, but at least no longer directly antagonistic; the actual use of compulsion on the part of superstructural enforcement agents might become less frequent; in the actual labour process, rules could become increasingly self-imposed, still the essential and irreducible feature of social life, but no longer regarded as an alien imposition. But these rules, the vehicle of social administration, would still be addressed to human beings; they, rather than things, would remain the proper object of administration.

4.3 KAMENKA AND TAY: 'BUREAUCRATIC-ADMINISTRATIVE REGULATION'

In their papers 'Beyond the French Revolution' (1971), 'Beyond bourgeois individualism' (1975) and 'Social traditions, legal traditions' (1980),[14] E. Kamenka and A. E. S. Tay have brought together Tönnies's *Gemeinschaft/Gesellschaft* distinction and Pashukanis's model of post-capitalist (post-legal) regulation. They have argued that Pashukanis's model should be seen as filling a lacuna in Tönnies's work, in so far as the *Gemeinschaft/Gesellschaft* distinction fails to pick out the form of social regulation increasingly prevalent in advanced industrial societies, namely the bureaucratic-administrative.[15] This form

> Seeks to regulate an activity and not to adjudicate in collisions between individuals; its fundamental concern is with consequences rather than with fault or *mens rea*, with public need or public interest, or the interest of the activity itself, rather than private rights and individual duties. (BBI, p. 139)

While in the atomized, post-*Gemeinschaft* world of bureaucratic-administrative regulation human beings present themselves as individuals, it is not as individual subjects of rights, but

> . . . as carrying out roles . . . as standing in defined 'vertical' relations of subordination and sub-subordination. (BFR, p. 135)

In schematic form, the bureaucratic-administrative model contrasts with the two poles of Tönnies's dichotomy as shown in table 4.2.

Table 4.2. The Kamenka-Tay Schema.

	Gemein-schaft	Gesell-schaft	*Bureaucratic-administrative*
(1) It elaborates and defends individual rights	No	Yes	No
(2) It confronts people in immediate, face-to-face relations	Yes	No	No
(3) It treats people as subjects	?	Yes	No
(4) Its overriding goal is social harmony	Yes	No	Yes

Though the schema is crude, it brings out features of Kamenka's and Tay's analyses which are important for this inquiry. The query concerning the subject/object distinction on the *Gemeinschaft* model suggests that that very distinction hardly arises in the intimacy of the pure *Gemeinschaft*.[16] Arguably, it is only with the emergence of the relatively sophisticated categories of rights, duties and responsibility that it becomes possible to distinguish between treating people as subjects and treating them as objects. The important insight of Kamenka and Tay is that the bureaucratic-administrative form negates the assertion of legal subjectivity at points where it might be defended, but where its defence would be administratively inconvenient.

In introducing and defending their typology, Kamenka and Tay have remained neutral on the question of whether or not it is proper to apply the term 'law' to all three models of regulation (BFR, pp. 136–7, STLT, p. 22). They have suggested that in one sense all three should be considered to be models of law, in so far as they are opposed to a fourth model, that of domination-submission, which is 'rule by terror and the imposition of force'. The latter is

> . . . clearly extra-legal and supra-legal in that it neither implies nor requires a structured system of regulation incorporating certain values and moral or socio-political assumptions. (BFR, p. 137)

But, in the light of this fourth distinction, it is not clear that bureaucratic-administrative regulation does, after all, have a stronger claim than domination-submission to be considered a separate form of *law*. *Gesellschaftlich* regulation depends on the assertion and defence of more or less individualistic rights and duties within a public coercive framework. *Gemeinschaftlich* regulation depends on a degree of consensus concerning social goals, combined with a relatively unchallenged allocation of social roles and rewards. But bureaucratic-administrative regulation embodies subordination and sub-subordination without either the guarantees of legal answerability proclaimed by the *Gesellschaft* or the guarantees of face-to-face moral pressure embodied in the *Gemeinschaft*. In so far as the bureaucratic-administrative model is distinct from the other two, it might be more perspicuous to see it as strictly non-legal, corresponding in its distinctive features, to the model of domination-submission. In many passages in their work, Kamenka and Tay have come near to acknowledging this, saying, for instance, that only *gesellschaftlich* law has 'a bias toward freedom and equality and against arbitrary coercion [through] the specificity of legal procedures, legal institutions and legal values' (STLT, p. 26). Having elaborated their third model to cover forms of social organization in advanced societies both capitalist and socialist, Kamenka and Tay have applied it differently in different papers, giving more emphasis to the Soviet case in BFR and to the west in BBI. They have demonstrated that in both societies typically bureaucratic-administrative values are widely pursued: the overriding of legal rights for policy goals; the distancing of administrators from subjects of administration; the reduction of individuals from subject to object status; the pursuit of an engineered consensus at the expense of political debate. In capitalist countries these are the characteristic procedures of government agencies and private corporations alike. In what respect, then, do they differ from their socialist counterparts? The difference that exists lies in the space left for contesting the power of those agencies from within the law. The extent of that space varies from country to country and is the outcome of the struggle waged by citizens, individually and in organizations, to impose legal answerability on the agents of power. At the present time, the control over information is perhaps the important stake in that struggle: access to information presently monopolized by the agents of power and the control of surveillance. This is a struggle to extend the space governed by legal-constitutional norms and to diminish that which lies in the bureaucratic-administrative domain, beyond the law.

This is observed most clearly by Hannah Arendt in her account of 'the transformation [sic] of government into administration, or of republics into bureaucracies': 'Bureaucracy is the form of government in which everybody is deprived of political freedom, of the power to act; for the rule by Nobody is not no-rule, and where all are equally powerless we have a tyranny without a tyrant'.[17] I would distance myself only from Hannah Arendt's terminology, since for me it is not bureaucracy that is undesirable, understood in the Weberian sense of a rationalized, centralized system of accounting and information. On the contrary, I have argued that such a system is an inseparable component of any high-technology society. What is undesirable is to allow the bureaucratic-administrative apparatus to operate beyond the bounds of the *Rechtsstaat*.

NOTES

1. See in particular sections III.1.4 and III.1.13 of that work and the introductory essay to the 1931 edition.
2. See section IV.3 of that work.
3. F. Tönnies, *On Sociology*, 1971 edition, pp. 9–10.

4. *Gemeinschaft ünd Gesellschaft*, 1969 edition, III.1.12, II.1.13, 111.1.14. Tönnies's analysis of these possibilities is rendered impenetrable in the English translation by two factors: First, since the translator has rendered *Gesellschaft* in the title of the book by 'association' and since *Gemeinschaft/Gesellschaft* are exclusive terms, it is paradoxical to find *gemeinschaftliche Bündnisverhältnisse* translated as 'associations of *Gemeinschaft*' (*Gemeinschaft und Gesellschaft*, p. 197, English translation, p. 222). But that confusion is a minor one. Second, and more seriously, in the concluding section on this topic (*GG*, III.1.14), the translator has systematically rendered *Verbindung* by 'association', thus masking the *Verbindung/Bündnisverhältnis* distinction which structures the passage.
5. *Gemeinschaft und Gesellschaft*, III.1.12.
6. Not all *gemeinschaftlich* relationships were authoritative for Tönnies. In the 1931 Introductory Article to *Gemeinschaft und Gesellschaft*, he distinguished another type of *gemeinschaftlich* relationship: the 'fellowship type'.
7. The increasing significance of freedom of contract and, particularly, of enabling laws which leave everything to 'free' agreement, implies a relative reduction of that kind of coercion which results from the threat of mandatory and prohibitory norms. Formally it represents, of course, a decrease of coercion. But it is also obvious how advantageous this state of affairs is to those who are economically in the position to make use of the empowerments. The exact extent to which the total amount of 'freedom' within a given legal community is actually increased depends entirely upon the concrete economic order and especially upon the property distribution. In no case can it be simply deduced from the content of the law. . .

   In a private economy, coercion is exercised to a consider able extent by the private owners of the means of production and acquisition, to whom the law guarantees their property and whose power can thus manifest itself in the competitive struggle of the market.

   . . . the more powerful party in the market, i.e. normally the employer, has the possibility to set the terms, to offer the job 'take it or leave it', and, given the normally more pressing economic need of the worker, to impose his terms upon him. . .

   This type of rules does no more than create the framework for valid agreements which, under conditions of formal freedom, are officially available to all. Actually, however, they are accessible only to the owners of property and thus in effect support their very autonomy and power positions. (Max Weber, *Economy and Society*, vol. 3, pp. 729–730)

8. Introductory Article to *Gemeinschaft und Gesellschaft*, English translation, p. 23.
9. C. Arthur, 'Towards a materialist theory of law', 1977, p. 31.
10. R. Sharlet, 'Pashukanis and the withering-away of law', 1978, p. 170.
11. Page references in the text in this section are to E.B. Pashukanis, *General Theory of Law and Marxism*.
12. Cf. Hart's *gesellschaftlich* account of rights in H.L.A. Hart, 'Bentham on legal rights', 1973, and its critique in N. MacCormick, 'Rights in Legislation', 1977.
13. R. Schlesinger, *Soviet Legal Theory*, 1945, pp. 161–2.
14. Page references in the text in this section are to Kamenka's and Tay's three papers, abbreviated BFR, BBI, STLT.
15. Cf. Talcott Parsons's criticism in 'Some afterthoughts on *Gemeinschaft* and *Gesellschaft*', pp. 153 ff.
16. The same was true of the distinction between law and morals in Tönnies's table of oppositions.
17. H. Arendt, *On Violence*, 1969, p. 81.

5

Experiments of Living

5.1 LIBERTARIANISM AND PLURALISM

Heir to the twin legacies of the Victorian era, liberalism and paternalism, and lacking formal constitutional principles, the English legal system has shown itself less than fully adequate to deal with two important problems of civil rights in recent years: the problem of information, in respect both of access to it by private citizens and of protection against its unauthorized transmission by public agencies; and the problem of increasing cultural and moral pluralism. Leaving the first problem to the next chapter, we shall reflect in the following pages on the juridical implications of Millian libertarianism.

John Stuart Mill said of his *Essay on Liberty* that it was 'likely to survive longer than anything else that I have written'[1] and, with all its rhetorical excesses and profound theoretical ambivalences, it has remained the inspiration of subsequent libertarians through to Wolfenden, Hart and Williams.[2] For Isaiah Berlin, notoriously, Mill was the spokesman of the 'negative' view of liberty, of liberty as the absence of obstacles to doing what you want.[3] Yet the dominant theme of the text is something positive: 'the importance to man and society of a large variety in types of character and of giving full freedom to human nature to expand itself in innumerable and conflicting directions'. It is of course true that for Mill the most important condition for attaining a free society is that there should be a minimum of 'interference' (a favourite Millian term) by the state in the citizen's organization of his or her own life. But to identify non-interference with liberty is to confuse a condition of liberty with the content of liberty itself. That content is expounded in chapters

2 and 3 of the *Essay*, 'Of the liberty of thought and discussion' and 'Of individuality, as one of the elements of wellbeing'. Against what he saw as the advancing tide of mediocrity and uniformity, Mill advocated diversity of life-styles, of 'different experiments of living' (p. 185).[4] Mill's manifesto is marked by a tension between two insights: first, that freedom can be valued as a prime utility only by a relatively advanced people; second, that the urgent need to defend freedom in modern times arises precisely from the danger posed by mass democracy to certain values, in particular the value of individualism. It is here that we can locate the target of Marx's hostility to Mill's political ideology and of subsequent Marxist critiques of individualistic libertarianism: given the historical context of massive inequalities of power within which liberal values were being asserted, the Millian position appeared to socialist critics to be the sheerest hypocrisy, a demand for sham individual freedom, as opposed to real social freedom, which could be attained only through revolutionary class struggle. We have noted already the dangers involved in this externalist approach to the liberal programme: the form/content vocabulary, in which liberalism is said to have a libertarian form and an exploitative content (the theme of the *Grundrisse* critique) can properly be turned against Marxists, in the accusation that communism has an emancipatory form and a manipulatory content. My thesis is that, at least in advanced societies, the two struggles are conjoined: on the one hand, the struggle to transform power relations between the classes, and, on the other hand, the struggle to give reality to individual, legally enforceable liberties. These two are related not as form and content, but as two components of one movement. The problematic nature of the libertarian component will be considered briefly in the following pages.

5.2. J. S. MILL'S THREE FORMULAE

Legislators seeking guidance in framing liberal statutes are confronted by three different formulations of the principle of freedom in Mill's text:

(1) . . . the sole end for which mankind are warranted, individually or collectively, in interfering with the liberty of action of any of their number, is self-protection . . . the only purpose for which power can be rightfully exercised over any member of a civilized community, against his will, is to prevent harm to others.

(2) His own good, either physical or moral, is not a sufficient warrant. He cannot rightfully be compelled to do or forbear because it will be better for him to do so, because it will make him happier, because, in the opinion of others, to do so would be wise, or even right . . . The only part of the conduct of anyone, for which he is amenable to society, is that which concerns others. In the part which merely concerns himself, his independence is, of right, absolute. Over himself, over his own body and mind, the individual is sovereign. (p. 135)

(3) The reason for not interfering, unless for the sake of others, with a person's voluntary acts, is consideration for his liberty. His voluntary choice is evidence that what he so chooses is desirable, or at least endurable, to him, and his good is on the whole best provided for by allowing him to take his own means of pursuing it. But by selling himself as a slave, he abdicates his liberty; he foregoes any future use of it beyond that single act. He therefore defeats, in his own case, the very purpose which is the justification of allowing him to dispose of himself . . . The principle of freedom cannot require that he should be free not to be free. It is not freedom to be allowed to alienate his freedom. (p. 236)

As a gloss to the third formulation, we could add:

If either a public officer or any one else saw a person attempting to cross a bridge which had been ascertained to be unsafe, and there were not time to warn him of his danger, they might seize him and turn him back, without any real infringement of his liberty; for liberty consists in doing what one desires, and he does not desire to fall into the river. (p. 229)

The same principle, Mill held, must be applied to consumer legislation, where *caveat emptor* must be tempered in the interests of public safety, allowing the legislator to enforce the labelling of dangerous drugs, since 'the buyer cannot wish not to know that the thing he possesses has poisonous qualities'.

At first sight, formulae (1) and (2) look like two statements of the same principle: indeed the sentences follow one another in the text. Both admonish the legislator to distinguish harm to others from harm to oneself, even though some actions, like setting fire to oneself in a department store, might involve both. But, as McCloskey has observed,[5] (1) is the condition of degree zero state intervention: it, taken on its own, allows for intervention only to prevent A from harming B. With the addition of (2), intervention is also allowed to force A to benefit B. In other words, according to both (1) and (2), the law can prevent A from murdering or robbing B, but only with the addition of (2) can it institute a system of income tax to redistribute wealth from A to B. Of modern political theorists, only Nozick, perhaps, is inclined to the zero option of (1), assuming that the raising of taxation to fund the police and armed forces can be seen as a means of institutionally guaranteeing the prevention of harms. It is significant that Mill immediately expanded (1) into (2), distancing himself within a paragraph from the extreme *laissez-faire* position of the zero option. The addition of (3) allows for the active role of the law as protector of the individual citizen against misinformation, or simply lack of information, on the part of private corporations and government agencies. Defenders of individual liberty will need more positive and specific principles, in particular Finnis's natural right not to be deliberately lied to, in order to make Mill's goal of pluralist freedom a reality.[6] Mill's principles give the legislator no hard and fast answers as to where to draw the line, but they advocate a presumption in favour of non-interference: in areas of life which are, *prima facie,* private, the burden of proof lies on the advocate of interference.

5.3 J. S. MILL AND THE LAW

Mill's defence of individual freedom, including the freedom of individuals to form their own groups and to engage in 'experiments of living' was coupled with a hostility towards governmental 'interference' and little interest in the systematic deployment of rights within a legal, constitutional framework which would give effect to those freedoms. The relative absence of law in England was for Mill a self-evident good, a good which was likely to fall victim to increasing democracy, the increasing identification of the individual with his government (*On Liberty*, p. 134). With excellent perceptiveness, Mill saw the dangerous ambiguity in the formulae of populist democracy, 'self government', 'the power of the people over themselves':

> The 'people' who exercise the power are not always the same people with those over whom it is exercised; and the 'self-government' spoken of is not the government of each by himself, but of each by all the rest. The will of the people, moreover, practically means the will of the most numerous or the most active *part* of the people; the majority, or those who succeed in making themselves accepted as the majority; the people, consequently *may* desire to oppress a part of their number; and precautions are as much needed against this as against any other abuse of power. (p. 129)

But, interestingly, he did not develop the idea of 'constitutional checks' further, just at the point when they would seem to be most crucially necessary. The reason is that Mill envisaged that two historical tendencies must intersect, such that the point in its development when 'a people' would value individual liberty highly enough to want to defend it, would be the point when constitutional guarantees would no longer be necessary:

> Liberty, as a principle, has no application to any state of things anterior to the time when mankind have become capable of being improved by free and equal discussion. (*On Liberty*, p. 136)

The vehicle for reaching that point was education, the high Victorian cultural vision that sat so uneasily with Mill's fear of the philistine masses' potential for submerging individuality and genius. Given an education based on utilitarian principles, the gap between *Gemeinschaft* and *Gesellschaft* would perhaps be narrowed to a point where egotism, and hence the need for constitutional guarantees, might wither away (*Utilitarianism*, p. 265).

Thus in his extended defence of the individual liberties which make up the good life, Mill made only passing references to the legal guarantees necessary for the defence of those liberties: a neglect which is continuous with the *gemeinschaftlich*, quasi-anarchist strain in his libertarianism. Most frequently, where law was mentioned in *On Liberty*, it was as an agency of repression of liberties.[7] Of course, the Millian formula for legitimate state intervention to curb an individual's behaviour, 'to prevent harm to others', coupled with the interdiction on intervention 'for his own good, either physical or moral' (p. 135), constituted the heart of a system of constitutional immunity rights. But the lack of any specific reference to the kind of legal order that would be needed to enforce those rights was a result of the utopian tendency of the *Essay on Liberty* to see laws as no more than potential restraints on liberty and individualism: the mirror image of the Marxist view that laws, in endorsing the undesirable individualism of capitalism, are subservient to the established order and impotent to bring about change. Mill did approve of institutions like trial by jury (*On Liberty*, p. 243), but as one of the 'questions of development . . . parts of national education', as a form of popular participation in legal decision making, rather than as a guarantee against law being used as an instrument of government.[8] In one particular case Mill did explicitly recognize the importance of law as an agent of change from the enforced *Gemeinschaft* of 'the almost despotic power of husbands over wives':

> . . . nothing more is needed for the complete removal of the evil than that wives should receive the protection of law in the same manner, as all other persons. (*On Liberty*, p. 238)

Mill's position on the relations between the sexes was, in this respect, clear. The law must first guarantee equality of legal rights, in particular property rights; and second, within that egalitarian framework, it must liberalize divorce, the alternative being domestic 'despotism'. He explicitly endorsed the use of law as an instrument of change when the present non-libertarian order of family despotism itself had the backing of law. But on the continued use of law to maintain the libertarian order, within the family as well as outside it, he was markedly silent. Here once again he was closer to the Marxist utopians and to the anarchists than one might have expected.

Mill spoke, on occasion, of the defence of an individual's legal rights, of the injustice of depriving 'any one of his personal liberty, his property, or any other thing which belongs to him by law' (*Utilitarianism*, p. 298), but the idea of a constitutional (let alone a natural or human) right would be sheer metaphysics for Mill, at least until it were given a translation into utilitarian terms: 'It is proper to state that I forego any advantage which could be derived from the idea of abstract right, as a thing independent of utility.' (p. 136)

Yet, within a relatively complex society, Millian freedoms must remain empty until they can be translated into rights within a system which allows persons to defend their freedoms against encroachments on them by governmental and corporate agencies. I shall argue later that in a complex society there must be laws protecting privacy and freedom of information, which can be effectively invoked by individuals if they are to be able to protect their rights. The alternatives are either to dismantle high technology (information production) or to hope – in utopian fashion – that it will not be used by those with access to it to anyone's detriment.

5.4 THE SOCIAL CONSTRUCTION OF PRIVACY AND HARM

If it is legitimate to enact and apply the criminal law in order to prevent an individual from harming others, but not, or at least not normally, to prevent him from harming himself, then the feasibility of applying that criterion of legitimacy will depend on being able to find a consensus with respect to its two components: first, the question of what constitutes privacy; second, the question of what constitutes harm.

First, how are we to determine the domain of the private?

> The distinction between the part of a person's life which concerns only himself, and that which concerns others, many persons will refuse to admit. How (it may be asked) can any part of the conduct of a member of society be a matter of indifference to the other members? No person is an entirely isolated being; it is impossible for

a person to do anything seriously or permanently hurtful to himself, without mischief reaching at least to his near connections, and often far beyond them. (p. 210–1)

In reply, Mill reverted to the distinction between disapproval and legal prevention. The former, he suggested, is appropriate for 'a man who causes grief to his family by addiction to bad habits' (p. 212), while the latter should be applied only to one who fails to perform 'some definite duty incumbent on him to the public'. This distinction, of course, leaves untouched the question of how to determine which duties should be public duties and which should be private or family duties. Mill ignored that question in an espousal of *Gesellschaftlichkeit* which is brutal and direct: 'No person ought to be punished simply for being drunk; but a soldier or policeman should be punished for being drunk on duty.' The misery caused to family members by an individual's drunkenness in private is an 'inconvenience [which] society can afford to bear, for the sake of the greater good of human freedom'. Here we find Mill explicitly weighing up the cost of lost *gemeinschaftlich* values: the result of his computation is never in doubt.

Yet, once it is recognized that the line between the public and the private domains is drawn according to social, not natural, standards, which themselves have both an historical evolution and a normative charge, Mill's formulations give only the most minimal guidance for the legislator. Let us reflect for a moment on a practice whose history is as long as the institution of marriage and whose popularity shows no signs of waning: adultery. In contrast to contemporary Saudi Arabia or Massachussets in 1948,[9] contemporary England regards adultery as a private activity with respect to the criminal law.[10] In this country, in other words, the sanctions of the criminal law are not invoked to prevent the practice. Yet few practices could be less 'self-regarding'. Adultery involves the deception of an individual by two others, frequently causing grief, pain and indignity. Its effects on other family members in many cases and, as an exemplar, on the institution of the family itself, are incalculable. Yet fraud in marraige is regarded by the criminal law as a private affair, in business as a public one. The reasons for this are complex. Economic factors include the transformation of the family in advanced capitalist societies from a central unit of production to a minimal unit of child care and socialization, whose maintenance as a unit is no longer based on an economic imperative. With the arrival of efficient methods of birth control, the freedom of women to organize their sexual lives without fear of unwanted pregnancy has altered the balance of power between the sexes. More generally, the fragmenting of traditional patriarchal relations has meant that rules previously reserved either *de jure*[11] or *de facto* for the restriction of women's freedom have given way to a greater sexual freedom for both sexes. The task of ordering these factors in an explanatory schema lies with historians and social scientists. For our purposes, the important lesson is just this: that to defend Mill's libertarian ideal, we must defend the right of individuals to direct or misdirect their own behaviour and relationships within a certain domain; yet the extent of that domain is determined not by nature but by an historico-normative process of social development, in which a publicly enforced *Gemeinschaft* dissolves into a plurality of *Gemeinschaften*. This is what Mill called 'the liberty . . . of combination among individuals; freedom to unite, for any purpose not involving harm to others' (p. 138). Yet this development is complex, uneven, irregular: not a linear progression of the simple replacement of one Tönniesean form by the other, but a shift in the balance of power between classes and between individual citizens, government agencies and private corporations.

At each stage in the changing relation between *Gemeinschaft* and *Gesellschaft*, the legal recognition of family ties, whether to 'privatize' or 'publicize' them, has been an important factor in social development. Kant's philosophy of law had mirrored a stage of evolution at which subordinate members of a household were deprived of full legal personality, yet sexual relations between husband and wife were modelled rather bizarrely on a pure *gesellschaftlich* contract. Hegel had reversed these two Kantian positions in his picture of legally atomized family structure, optimistically held together by love, not contract. While for Mill, as we have seen already, 'the almost despotic power of husbands over wives' (p. 238) was still a reality which could be changed only by extending the same legal rights to wives 'as to all other persons'. But just how far family relations should be made over to the pure *Gesellschaft* is a question on which advocates of civil rights are not unanimous. As Kamenka and Tay observe:

> The conversion of the law of matrimonial offences into family law and all it implies has proceeded rapidly in the West; the accompanying institution of the informal Family Court is being experimented with in Poland. (The Polish decision to have assaults within the family dealt with within the Family Court represents a consistent extension of the *Gemeinschaft* ideology enshrined in the concept of family law; interestingly, those who promote women's and children's rights in Western society particularly want such assaults dealt with by the ordinary courts on *Gesellschaft* principles.) ('Social traditions, legal traditions', p. 25)

Second, how are we to determine what constitutes harm? What counts as harm varies from epoch to epoch and from culture to culture. The libertarian legislator operates within an historical context which he can modify, but not ignore. Beyond preventible physical harm to individuals and sets of individuals lies the problematic area of moral harm, and here it is impossible to pick out a simple, unidirectional line in recent legislation. In many cases a complex balance has to be struck between different kinds of harm and between the conflicting interests of the different groups affected. The Race Relations Act (1976) amends the Public Order Act (1936) by prohibiting 'incitement to racial hatred', so that:[12]

> A person commits an offence if –
> (a) he publishes or distributes written matter which is threatening, abusive or insulting; or
> (b) he uses in any public place or at any public meeting words which are threatening, abusive or insulting,
> in a case where, having regard to all the circumstances, hatred is likely to be stirred up against any racial group in Great Britain by the matter or words in question.

Here then the application of 'harm' is explicitly extended to make criminal 'abusive and insulting' behaviour of a racial kind.

In the sphere of sexual morality, on the other hand, the thrust of Millian libertarianism has been in the opposite direction: against a background of paternalist authoritarianism, the libertarian consensus until recently advocated the extension of the domain of the private, on the assumption that any 'harms' resulting from that extension were trivial or, at least, ones which 'society can afford to bear'. But that assumption has, of late, been subjected to criticism from what can loosely be termed 'the left' and 'the right'.

From 'the left', it has been argued that pornography, in so far as it degrades women, 'could be regarded as a social harm'.[13] But the Williams Report suggests that, although many in the women's movement shared that view, only a few thought that it provided grounds for the legal prohibition of pornography, either because they saw pornography as merely a symptom (and a relatively unimportant one) of deeper social attitudes which would not be affected by such legislation, or because they 'tended to attach greater importance to freedom of expression than to the need to suppress pornography'.

From 'the right', it has been argued that 'the proliferation of pornography results in increasing sexual offences',[14] i.e. to behaviour agreed on all sides to be harmful, in particular to rape and other kinds of sexual violence. After considering the available evidence, from psychologists, sociologists, statisticians and others, the Williams Committee concluded that, while absolute certainty was impossible, the balance of the evidence went against that view. The case for a causal connection between pornography and sexual violence was, according to the Committee, flimsy. This section of the Report is disturbing even (or perhaps especially) for the committed libertarian: for the burden of proof is shifted on to the conservative critics of pornography in a way that the libertarian would be loath to generalize. For instance, in the case of a pharmaceutical product suspected of being a potential health hazard, he, as a libertarian, would want to see the burden placed squarely on the manufacturers and distributors of the product.

As a bearer of *gesellschaftlich* libertarian values, the Williams Committee refused to engage in broader questions of 'cultural pollution, moral deterioration and the undermining of human compassion, social values and basic institutions' by pornography. The prevention or control of those forms of 'harm' did not come within its terms of reference.[15] 'Harm', in the tradition within which the Committee was working covers what is actually or potentially physically damaging and what is psychologically or morally offensive to individuals.[16] How to test for 'offensiveness' is a difficult question. If 'distaste' is the criterion, then, as Mill observed, not all distaste is allowed to count:

> There are many who consider as an injury to themselves any conduct which they have a distaste for, and resent it as an outrage to their feelings; . . . But there is no parity between the feeling of a person for his own opinion, and the feeling of another who is offended at his holding it; no more than between the desire of a thief to take a purse, and the desire of the right owner to keep it. (p. 215)

Hart pointed out that the same distinction must apply for the libertarian even when awareness of the behaviour causes the cognizant individual not just distaste, but even distress:[17]

> If distress incident to the belief that others are doing wrong is harm, so also is the distress incident to the belief that others are doing what you do not want them to do. To punish people for causing this form of distress would be tantamount to punishing them simply because others object to what they do; and the only liberty that could coexist with this extension of the utilitarian principle is liberty to do those things to which no one seriously objects.

The Williams Committee applied this principle consistently, in recommending that the display of pornographic material, which could be (publicly) offensive, should be more strictly controlled, but that the law controlling the (private) availability of such material should be liberalized. Like Mill and Hart, the Committee stood by an intuitive distinction between the public and the private and refused to allow the term 'harm' to be extended to cases where one individual is upset by the mere knowledge that another individual is behaving in a particular fashion.[18]

While endorsing this libertarian tradition, I would distance myself from Mill, Hart and Williams in underlining its historical and cultural specificity. For, in a religious, traditional culture, the libertarian distinctions might simply not hold. There, the idea of 'pollution', marginalized in the Williams *Gesellschaft*, might be of central importance. In the *Gesellschaft*, it is indeed possible to distinguish sharply between being confronted by a public display of improper conduct, which provides legitimate grounds for complaint about offensiveness, and being merely cognizant that such conduct is taking place in private, which provides no such grounds. But in the traditional society such a distinction might either not be drawn at all, or, if drawn, it might mark out different points on the spectrum of acceptable/unacceptable behaviour. In such a society, the mere fact that a person was performing a certain act could constitute a pollution to society as a whole and hence cause it 'harm': the question of who was 'offended' by such an act, of whether it was done in public or in private, would be of secondary importance. Pollution of the ritual, ethical environment would be as 'objective' a fact as the pollution of the water supply.[19]

The emphasis on that specificity does not entail wholesale relativism, for two reasons. First, as I argue elsewhere, the minimal rational kernel of Marxist historicism should be preserved. Thus certain ways of living one's society become untenable under the impact of secularization and scientific ideology.[20] Categories of ritual pollution, properly constitutive of traditional, religious belief systems, cannot be resuscitated after the universalization of *gesellschaftlich* values.[21] Second, in avoiding ethnocentricity, in avoiding the trap of eternalizing and universalizing our own particular value system, we do not thereby deprive our own normative conclusions of their validity: we merely recognize irreducible plurality of ways of endowing the world with meaning. Against arch-rationalists, I maintain a scepticism concerning the place of reason in deciding between different horizons of social meaning.

5.5 ENFORCING THE *GEMEINSCHAFT*: LORD DEVLIN

In his criticism of the Millian libertarian assumptions of the Wolfenden Committee, whose *Report on Homosexual Offences and Prostitution* appeared in 1957, Lord Devlin argued as follows:[22]

(1) A society is justified in taking those steps necessary to ensure its survival.
(2) The maintenance and enforcement of an established morality is necessary to ensure a society's survival.
(3) Therefore a society is justified in maintaining and enforcing an established morality.

Up to this point in the argument, the libertarian has no reason to disagree with Lord Devlin, since he too holds that a degree of consensus, of agreement on social goals and standards, is necessary for the working of a *Rechtsstaat,* within which libertarian values can be defended. But Devlin proceeded from (3) to a further conclusion, to which the libertarian will not follow him:

(4) Therefore it is not possible to set theoretical limits to the power of the state to legislate against immorality.

Now (4) does not follow from (3), on the libertarian reading of (3), because, for the libertarian, the 'established morality' is precisely a consensus or agreement that certain types of behaviour should be immune to legal interference. One important reason, for the libertarian, why we owe allegiance to the legal system as a whole is that it defends a domain of privacy which, it is generally agreed, should remain inviolate. Thus, as Hart has pointed out, Devlin's crowning slogan 'it is no more possible to define a sphere of private morality than . . . one of private subversive activity' (p. 77) trades on a specious parallel. For 'private subversive activity' is a contradiction in terms, whereas 'private morality' is not.[23] Homosexuality, for instance, can be legislated into being subversive: when illegal, it gives grounds for blackmail and so becomes a component part of treason.

Devlin's espousal of the enforceable *Gemeinschaft* obliges the libertarian to sharpen his position in two respects:

First, he must assert the explicitly *gesellschaftlich* view that morality is not a 'seamless web'. On the contrary, there are cut-off points between different areas of life of an individual or a group, allowing for the preservation of certain areas of inviolable privacy.

Second, he must agree that there is no area of life which is absolutely beyond the law, in the elementary sense that there are legal codes which intervene in areas the libertarian regards as private: notoriously the 1949 Prohibition of Mixed Marriage Act and the 1950 Immorality Act in South Africa. The application of the public/private distinction is socially determined, varying sometimes radically from society to society, from age to age. But he need not conclude from that that his society is not justified in asserting a particular application. The law of a constitutional state is self-referring and self-binding, establishing areas of life into which the law cannot intervene: devotion to that constitutional principle is part of the 'established morality' of advanced societies.

This schematic counter-claim ignores the tension with Devlin's position between two themes: the explicit commitment to individual liberty, both as a normative principle of legislation (p. 79) and as a reflection of an historical tendency, not easily reversed (p. 81), and the appeal to direct popular endorsement of the legal order by 'the man in the jury box' (p. 78), whose instincts on particular issues may run counter to libertarian principles. The tension is a direct reflection of the missing level in the English constitutional system: the level of self-binding constitutional limitations, which allow for the deflection of particular prejudices without despotic imposition. This does not mean, of course, that the formal presence of constitutional limitations in itself guarantees substantive personal liberties. Just as, in Devlin's description of the English, informal mode of development, 'the limits of tolerance shift' (p. 81), so, in a more hierarchical constitutional order, the application of constitutional limitations shifts.[24] While constitutionality is not the magic key to the *Rechtsstaat*, its presence makes the mediation between democracy and libertarianism possible.

NOTES

1. J.S. Mill, *Autobiography*, 1971 edition, p. 150: Mill thought his *Logic* would also last.
2. *Report of the Committee on Homosexual Offences and Prostitution*, Cmnd. no. 247 (1957), the Wolfenden Report. H.L.A. Hart, *Law, Liberty and Morality*, 1963. *Report of the Committee on Obscenity and Film Censorship*, Cmnd. no. 7772 (1979), the Williams Report.
3. I. Berlin, *Two Concepts of Liberty*, 1958.
4. All page references to Mill in this chapter are to the Fontana collection *Utilitarianism, On Liberty*, 1962.
5. H.J. McCloskey, *J.S. Mill: a Critical Study*, 1971, pp. 106 ff.
6. J. Finnis, *Natural Law and Natural Rights*, 1980, p. 225.
7. See *On Liberty*, p. 141–2, on the iniquity of the 'Government Press Prosecutions of 1858'.
8. See E.P. Thompson, 'The state versus its "enemies"', in *Writing by Candlelight*, pp. 108–9. For Thompson, the jury is the place where the 'bargain between the law and the people . . . is struck'.
9. See H.L.A. Hart, *Law, Liberty and Morality*, p. 27.
10. Though adultery is still a component part of the first of the five 'facts' which a petitioner may adduce as causing the 'irretrievable breakdown' of the marriage, according to the Matrimonial Causes Act (1973). That first 'fact' now comprises 'two limbs': 'that the respondent has committed adultery and that the petitioner finds it intolerable to live with him'. In this sense, adultery still has a public role to play in the civil divorce proceeedings, even if banished from the criminal law. (P.M. Bromley, *Family Law*, 1981, pp. 195 ff.) On the evolution of the idea of privacy and attempts to define and defend it legally, see P. Stein and P. Shand, *Legal Values in Western Society*, chapter 8.
11. See P.M. Bromley, *Family Law*, pp. 187–8 for a summary of this historical development.
12. D.J. Walker and M.J. Redman, *Racial Discrimination*, 1977, p. 215.
13. Williams Report, p. 88.
14. Ibid., p. 61.
15. Ibid., p. 92.
16. Following Mill's lead, the Committee restricted itself to the harms prohibited by the criminal law, ignoring the complex array of torts actionable in civil law.

17. H.L.A. Hart, *Law, Liberty and Morality*, p. 47.
18. Naturally, any system of restriction must involve some phenomena which themselves could, indirectly, offend someone. Thus pornography might be legitimately sold (as we shall propose) in shops which announced their nature but did not allow their contents to be seen from the outside. The presence of such shops is something which itself could be found offensive by someone; we have indeed received complaints about shops of some such kind (though we cannot be sure how reticent the particular examples may have been). If there were no such shops, but only mail-order distributors, then the advertisements for these, even if they displayed no material, would certainly be found offensive. If one goes all the way down this line, however, one arrives at the situation in which people objected to even knowing that pornography was being read in private; and if one accepted as a basis for coercing one person's actions, the fact that others would be upset even by the thought of his performing those actions, one would be denying any substantive individual liberty at all. (Williams Report, pp. 99–100)
19. The total schematism of this unwonted excursion into armchair anthropology is as obvious as it is inexcusable. Evidently 'traditional' cultures, in which ritual pollution is an important fact may also maintain a highly formalized stratification between places which are and places which are not subject to pollution (see Mary Douglas, *Purity and Danger*, 1970, *passim*). The point of the excursion is simply to contrast the different role of individuals' responses in the two schematic cultures.
20. See B. Williams, 'The truth in relativism', 1981, p. 140.
21. Cf. C. Taylor, 'Rationality', 1982.
22. Lord Patrick Devlin, 'Morals and the criminal law' in R. Dworkin (ed.), *Philosophy of Law*, 1977. Page references in this section are to that paper.
23. H.L.A. Hart, 'Immorality and treason' in R. Dworkin (ed.), *Philosophy of Law*, p. 86.
24. See R. Dworkin, 'Constitutional Cases' in *Taking Rights Seriously*, 1977.

6

Towards a *Rechtsstaat*

6.1 *RECHTSSTAAT* AND DESPOTISM

In this chapter, we shall bring to the surface the theme which has so far lain submerged: the connection between law and political power, in particular between constitutionality and democracy, and the possibility of protecting our liberties in an advanced technological society. To get our bearings, we shall start with one of Isaiah Berlin's more notorious contentions, that 'there is no necessary connexion between individual liberty and democratic rule', indeed that connection 'is a good deal more tenuous than it seemed to many advocates of both'.[1] Berlin's reiterated theme, that in the plurality of social values a choice has constantly to be made between fundamentally incompatible goals, that a state of harmonization and synthesis of all values is mythical, has been endorsed in my account of the *Gemeinschaft/Gesellschaft* couple and will be asserted again in this chapter: some values can, indeed, be acquired only at the expense of others. Berlin was not, of course, arguing directly for incompatibility in his famous lecture, but simply for the absence of a necessary connection which the writers of eighteenth century Declarations of Rights were tempted to assume. At first glance, then, he was providing no more than a rapid résumé of Mill's *On Liberty*. But when we compare the résumé with the original, we find an important shift of emphasis. Mill had outlined a relatively complex historical story in which individual rights were first asserted as particular immunities against inroads by despotic power, then later (in the case of some countries) generalized by 'the establishment of constitutional checks'. At this stage of development:[2]

. . . mankind were content to combat one enemy by another, and to be ruled by a master, on condition of being guaranteed more or less efficaciously against his tyranny.

At this stage Mill envisaged a certain balance between individual liberties and restrained despotism, such that 'even despotism does not produce its worst effects, so long as individuality exists under it'.[3]

But all this, for Mill, was for very specific historical reasons. So long as people see power as being imposed on them from outside or from above, by despotic rule, they are likely to identify the struggle for democracy with the struggle for individual liberty (in so far as the despot denies the first and fails formally to guarantee the second). It is only when democracy has to some degree been attained that the danger of undervaluing individual liberty arises:[4]

As the struggle proceeded for making the ruling power emanate from the periodical choice of the ruled, some persons began to think that too much importance had been attached to the limitation of the power itself. *That* (it might seem) was a resource against rulers whose interests were habitually opposed to those of the people. What was now wanted was, that the rulers should be identified with the people; that their interest and will should be the interest and will of the nation. The nation did not need to be protected against its own will. There was no fear of its tyrannising over itself.

But nowhere in *On Liberty* did Mill suggest that the *risk* of the tyranny of the majority would justify a retreat from democracy to despotism. On the contrary, his view was that contemporary England was 'a state of society in which the labouring classes are avowedly treated as children or savages' and in which 'because the institutions . . . are a mass of inconsistencies . . . things find admittance into our practice which belong to the system of despotic, or what is properly called paternal, government'.[5] There was no hint of Berlin's romantic hankering for 'the Prussia of Frederick the Great or . . . the Austria of Josef II'.

Berlin's 'argument' for the divorce between political and personal liberty was somewhat bizarre. We can, he said:[6]

> . . . give valid reasons for saying that the average subject of the King of Sweden is, on the whole, a good deal freer today than the average citizen of the Republic of Rumania.

And, since Sweden is freer than Rumania, a kingdom is freer than a republic, so a despotism is freer than a democracy. The absurdity of this inference hardly needs to be pointed out. The example merely points to what is common knowledge: that democracy can be enjoyed in a constitutional monarchy and that a 'people's democracy' can systematically negate *both* democracy, institutional participation of the people in government, *and* individual liberties, the institutional defence of individuals' lives against government control.

Berlin's example, in fact, points in quite the opposite direction, since it supports rather than negates the thesis that democratic institutions and respect for individual freedom, far from being incompatible (or even rarely associated) are closely interconnected components of a single system.

Historically, the struggles in seventeenth century England to establish the basis of the *Rechtsstaat* embodying elements of personal freedom through rules of procedural justice in the law courts did in fact converge with the struggles to overthrow political absolutism.

Berlin might have found a better example of his thesis in a colonial regime like Hong Kong. There, it might be argued, a system of political absolutism, an absence, at any rate, of forms of parliamentary democracy, underwrites a system of formal and substantive rights for individuals, which can be asserted and enforced in the law courts. Berlin's view, extrapolated from his comments in *Two Concepts of Liberty*, might be that the Hong Kong model would most effectively preserve individuals' negative freedoms, with the inherited traditions of the common law untainted by the busybodying interventionist legislation encountered in tiresome welfare states, which would seem to be the result of popular participation in legislation.

But it would be strange to imagine the Hong Kong model existing in isolation, instead of as a transplant from a source where the two components of the *Rechtsstaat* coexist and reinforce one another via the imperfect interplay of the relatively independent branches of legislative, executive and judiciary. E. P. Thompson pictures trial by jury as a public playing out (test of reality) of legal rights, the point where individual persons claim to be treated as bearers of rights, not as administrative units. In a sovereign democracy, 'the people' is also responsible, if indirectly, for the content of laws through the legislative process. According to this crude model, the people has two points of entry into the system: the point of judicial process and the point of legislation. In a system where the people is represented only at the first level (the Hong Kong model), individuals' legal rights are always dependent on an authority over which they have little, if any, control. The guarantor of individual legal rights in such a system is external: the Governor, as representative of the British sovereign power. The final guarantee of the Hong Kong compromise is thus an approximation to a *Rechtsstaat* (a democratically endorsed system of rights) existing outside it.

So, unless the guarantee of individuals' rights lies artificially outside the system, a constitutional system must be self-referring and self-justifying. The guarantee of citizens' rights has to be embodied in a self-imposed constitution and the guarantor must owe his legitimate independence from the legislative and the executive to popular endorsement. Thus a constitution can and should contain limiting clauses on the type of legislation that can properly be enacted. It can contain articles which limit constitutional amendment and which refer to the purposes of the constitution and to its misuse. This is true of the German *Grundgesetz*, which 'can be amended only by laws which expressly amend or supplement the text thereof' (Art. 79) and may not 'be amended nor repeated nor suspended' in a state of emergency (Art. 81). Article 18 states that an individual who abuses his constitutional rights 'in order to combat the free basic democratic order' forfeits them. Article 20 ('unique in all written constitutions')[7] even authorizes resistance to 'any person or persons seeking to abolish the constitutional order, should no other remedy be possible'.

The idea that the people has two points of entry into the *Rechtsstaat*, a judicial point and a political-legislative point, is a normative goal (utopian for left critics), realized more or less successfully in different societies. Where power is as unequally divided as it is in the United Kingdom, where government and civil service secrecy is part of the political tradition and minimally controlled by law, access to the decision-making mechanisms is difficult for most citizens and popular control over the content of legislation is often weak and indirect, if not wholly absent. Moreover, in the absence of a Bill of Rights, it is easy for a government to overrule constitutional precedent[8] and it is difficult for citizens to assert (even formally) claims for what are elsewhere their entrenched rights.[9]

Mill's thought that 'even despotism does not produce its worst effects so long as individuality exists under it'[10] applies at best to the lot of particular sets of individuals in particular historical periods: *par excellence* to the intellectuals in eighteenth and nineteenth century absolutist states, particularly Russia, whose culture is rightly dear to Berlin and Nabokov. There is a sense too in which the freedoms defended by English common law coexisted with political absolutism and were even maintained by it in times of extreme reaction,[11] but it would be odd to maintain that that coexistence was other than a moment of struggle and tension, for the individual rights won by the common people were wrested from the unwilling but disunited hands of the established powers.

More important for our purposes, it would be not just romantic but positively dangerous to think that, in an age of advanced information technology, despotism would hold back from negating civil liberties in the absence of the political checks on its power which are maintained, however inefficiently, in what we call democracies. The age of bumbling, inefficient autocracy, allowing Oblomovs to flourish within it, if it ever existed outside literature, has gone for ever.

6.2 LAW AND LEGITIMACY

If the constitutional values of the *Rechtsstaat* need democratic endorsement in order to flourish, we must inquire into the political and ideological conditions for that endorsement to be a reality.

Hart and the 'internal point of view'

Over twenty years after its publication, Hart's *Concept of Law* still stands as one of the subtlest extended reflections on the problem of legitimacy. Hart has been categorized as a 'positivist' in the anthologies and he himself accepted that label, albeit with caution and a battery of distinctions.[12] In fact, as we shall see, Hart's position was more fully infused with an implicit political theory than he himself ever acknowledged and, for that reason, the purity of its positivism was fatally compromised.

To summarize the originality of Hart's position in a sentence: he attempted (1) to distinguish the behaviour of 'following a rule', by virtue of the 'internalization' of the rule system by the agent; (2) to distinguish advanced legal systems from other systems of rules by virtue of their hierarchical character, primary rules of the system gaining their validity through their relationship to the secondary rules; (3) to give a complex (and politically highly ambivalent and un-positivist) account of the validity of a legal system as a whole in terms of a fusion of (1) and (2), the 'internalization' of the secondary or basic rules of the system as a whole by some or all of the citizens.

With engaging freshness and lack of references to the sociological and philosophical classics, Hart set himself the task of discovering the *Erklären/Verstehen* distinction *de novo* within the context of jurisprudence. Peter Winch had already naturalized the distinction into English in his *Idea of a Social Science* (1958), where he had distinguished the domains of the natural and the human in terms of their objects, the contexts in which those objects are encountered and the mode of explanation appropriate to them, as shown in table 6.1.

While the positivist caricature of natural science represented by the left-hand side of table 6.1 is now part of the museum of philosophy, and while the very division itself, if it were to be usable, would need to be posed with precision, rather than as a slogan, the right-hand side of the table still contains material whose importance for jurisprudence is inescapable.

Table 6.1. The Erklären/Verstehen *Distinction in its Winchian Form.*

	Natural	Human
Objects	(1) Events governed by causal laws	(1) Actions governed by reasons: *zweckrational*
Contexts	(2) Systems of interacting forces	(2) Systems of meanings and rules
Explanation yielding	(3) Statistical probabilities	(3) Understanding for the interpreter identifying meanings etc.

Kelsen had already expressed the distinction with characteristic clarity and dogmatism in the *General Theory*:[13]

> The law of nature establishes that if *A* is, *B* is (or will be). The rule of law says: If *A* is, *B* ought to be. The rule of law is a norm (in the descriptive sense of that term). The meaning of the connection established by the law of nature between two elements is the 'is', whereas the meaning of the connection between two elements established by the rule of law is the 'ought'. The principle according to which natural science describes its object is causality; the principle according to which the science of law describes its object is normativity.

In Weber, Kelsen and Winch, the *Erklären/Verstehen* (causality/normativity) distinction had served to mark off different orders of discourse, of explanation, of objects and of connections between objects. For Winch, the key to human interaction is its 'point or meaning', in other words the combination of intentions and rules.

While rules cannot be understood in the absence of social intentions, intentionality in turn presupposes the existence of rule-governed institutions, establishing internal relations between crime and punishment, buying and selling, etc. The two aspects of social behaviour, at least of relatively sophisticated social behaviour, are summarized in Weber's formula: 'meaningful behaviour oriented according to expectations stemming from rules'.

Martin Hollis illustrates the connection between the two aspects like this:[14]

> Rules do, no doubt, shape action in tangible or psychological ways. But, more to the point, they also govern the stock of available actions. When we said before that the criteria of sameness and difference depend on intentions, we were speaking of token actions. Tokens are tokens of a type and sameness and difference for types of action depend on rules. Whether a token V-sign is a rude gesture depends on the actor's intention but the actor needs to borrow from a stock, if he is to succeed in being rude in this way.
>
> What identifies a flick of the hand as a gesture of greeting or the sign of the cross as a blessing also thereby explains something. The rules of a ceremony include the gestures to be made; to know what the gestures are is to know which ceremony it is. There is a rule because a departure from the usual practice is not so much a rarity as a breach.

Thus, whatever the shortcomings of the distinction and the dualism that underlies it, as a dimension of human behaviour, the difference between a 'breach' of rules and a 'rarity' in a pattern (between breaking a rule and breaking a record) is irreducible.

Hart distinguished the 'external' from the 'internal' point of view in terms of different ways in which one may be 'concerned with the rules': 'either as an observer who does not himself accept them, or as a member of the group which accepts and uses them as guides to conduct' (p. 86).[15] The external observer, said Hart, in a memorable image, would be like

> . . . one who, having observed the working of a traffic signal in a busy street for some time, limits himself to saying that when the light turns red there is a high probability that the traffic will stop. He treats the light merely as a natural *sign that* people will behave in certain ways, as clouds are a *sign that* rain will come. In so doing he will miss out a whole dimension of the social life of those whom he is watching, since for them the red light is not merely a sign that others will stop: they look upon it as a *signal for* them to stop, and so a reason for stopping in conformity to rules which make stopping when the light is red a standard of behaviour and an obligation. (pp. 87–8)

For Hart, the external observer would be able to

> . . . record the regularities of observable behaviour and predict with a fair measure of success, and to assess the chances that a deviation from the group's normal behaviour will meet with hostile reaction or punishment. (p. 87)

But something would be missing from his behaviour. What? At one level, the passage from 'sign' to 'signal' can be read as a process of acceptance in a politically neutral sense, continuous with Kelsen's, Winch's and ultimately Weber's, analogous to the process in which a child learns to play a game, first by imitating the moves of others, then mastering and applying the rules himself, internalizing them and making them his own. In this politically neutral sense, there would be no suggestion that the individual who has mastered the rules of the game has endorsed those rules in any sense other than that he has decided to play the game, can distinguish breaches of its rules as breaches and penalties as penalties for those breaches. It is that understanding and mastery of systems of internal relations that constitutes the internal point of view for agents in all social interaction.

But Hart was not content to limit himself to that neutral sense of 'acceptance' in his treatment of the existence criteria (a) for a legal system and (b) for 'a healthy society' (p. 113), 'a society with law' (p. 197).

(a) *The existence criteria of a legal system*
In the Hartian epigram:

> There are . . . two minimum conditions necessary and sufficient for the existence of a legal system. On the one hand those rules of behaviour which are valid according to the system's ultimate criteria of validity must be generally obeyed, and, on the other hand, its rules of recognition specifying the criteria of legal validity and its rules of change and adjudication must be effectively accepted as common public standards of official behaviour by its officials.

Here a strong distinction is made between the 'officials' and the 'citizens': for a legal system to 'exist', the former must 'accept' the secondary rules, while the latter must simply 'obey' the primary rules and 'acceptance' is to be gauged in terms of motives. 'Citizens'' motives are a matter of indifference:

The first condition is the only one which private citizens *need* satisfy: they may obey each 'for his part only' and from any motive whatever; though in a healthy society they will in fact often accept these rules as common standards of behaviour and acknowledge an obligation to obey them, or even trace this obligation to a more general obligation to respect the constitution.

But 'officials'' motives are not:

The second condition must also be satisfied by the officials of the system. They must regard these as common standards of official behaviour and appraise critically their own and each other's deviations as lapses. Of course it is also true that besides these there will be many primary rules which apply to officials in their merely personal capacity which they need only obey. (p. 113)

Here Hart was using 'acceptance' in the politically committed sense, implying a particular, though inexplicit, political position, which could be labelled 'legal élitism'. Hart was tying the 'existence of a legal system' to the attitudes of a particular section of society, the 'officials', to their endorsement of the constitutional order as a whole.[16] The attitude of 'citizens' was held to be irrelevant to that question, though residually relevant to questions about the existence of a 'healthy society'.

The introduction of motives into the conception of acceptance, takes it beyond the neutral sense in which the bridge player understands the rules of the game, both primary and secondary, as rules and is able to apply them consistently and skilfully. The bridge player's motives are irrelevant to formal questions concerning his mastery of the rules of the game, just as they are irrelevant to the formal question of whether officials and/or citzens have understood the nature (criteria of validity, etc.) of the laws of the land and have correctly applied them. In preserving this politically neutral sense of the term 'acceptance', Hart would have remained true to the positivist programme of describing the formal criteria of the existence of a legal system, in isolation from any normative questions of political endorsement of the constitutional order. In this respect Hart's position would have been continuous with

Kelsenian positivism, which would exclude all considerations of attitudes (whether an endorsement or rejection) from pure jurisprudence.[17]

(b) *The existence criteria of a 'society with law'*

A society with law contains those who look upon its rules from the internal point of view as accepted standards of behaviour, and not merely as reliable predictions of what will befall them, at the hands of officials, if they disobey. But it also comprises those upon whom, either because they are malefactors or mere helpless victims of the system, these legal standards have to be imposed by force or threat of force; they are concerned with the rules merely as a source of possible punishment. (p. 197)

The sociological-political undertone here is more explicit. The 'society with law' contains non-officials (citizens) who share the internal point of view of the officials and their presence makes the society more 'stable': without them, the society will 'be made continually more repressive and unstable with the latent threat of upheaval'. But whether the 'society with law' contains these committed citizens necessarily or merely contingently is not clear.

The ambivalence between the neutral and the committed senses of 'acceptance' (in MacCormick's phrase the confusion of a 'distinction between levels of understanding' and a distinction 'between levels of volitional commitment')[18] should be avoided because it introduces the question of endorsement at a point where it is not required. If committed acceptance of the constitutional order by officials were required for the existence of a legal system, then one would have to exclude from the class of legal systems those systems holding in dependent, non-sovereign territories, where the local officials did not extend a politically committed acceptance to the given legal order, yet administered it efficiently, consistently and in accordance with procedural justice, adopting the neutral acceptance of the expert, but uninterested, card player. The reply to that objection might be that the key to the legality of such a dependent territory would lie in the committed acceptance of the constitutional norms of the sovereign territory, by the officials of the sovereign territory, and that, in so far as that commitment were not endorsed, at one remove, by the officials of the dependent territory, then the dependent territory would, indeed, not have a legal system in the full sense of the word.

But the more important lesson of this close reading of Hart is that his rather shadowy (b) conception, that of 'a society with law', which, ideally, embodies both a democratic distribution of rights and a democratic endorsement of the legal system, in other words a full social *Rechtsstaat*, can be described only in terms which are rather resistant to formal analysis. In other words, the question whether or not a particular order embodies a *Rechtsstaat* may be less easy to answer in polar (yes/no) terms than the formal question whether or not it embodies a legal system.[19]

Nonetheless, in sketching the lineaments of (b) and in making the distinction between (a) and (b) visible, Hart reopened the question of legitimacy which pure positivism appeared to have closed.

Marxism, ideology and legitimacy

Althusser

Constitutionality and legitimacy are connected through the contentious category of the subject. In Marxist critiques of ideology, and most sharply in Althusser's interventions,[20] that category is held to have a function only in ideological, not in scientific, discourse. The examples Althusser adduced are of religious and legal practice, in which individuals, in virtue of participating in the given rituals, present themselves as subjects, a mixed juridico-philosophical category, comprising consciousness, freedom and the capacity to assume responsibility for action. In class societies, according to this familiar model, that self-presentation is illusory, or, in Althusser's correction of the traditional formula, it is an 'imaginary relation to real relations' (p. 156). It is seen to be imaginary because (1) it presupposes an 'imaginary' liberty of action relative to the 'real', material determinants of the production relations, and (2) science has as its object structures consisting of sets of relations, whose terms are 'bearers', not subjects. The shortcomings of this picture, both of the nature of science, and of the relation between structure and practice, need not detain us here. What I wish to salvage from it is the thought that 'ideology is eternal' (p. 164) and universal, in that 'there are practices only through the mediation of ideology' (p. 159), that is through the mediation of subjects, and 'individuals are always-already subjects'. Subjectivity, then, is not eliminable, as some scientistic reductionisms would hold. In so far as a rational agent adopts an internal point of view towards his own actions, regarding them as *his* actions, and his commitments as *his* commitments, he is acting in the mode of the subject, even though, as the classic Marxist ideology critique shows, that asserted autonomy may be constrained within the narrowest bounds determining the possible objects of choice and modes of commitment. Nonetheless, within those bounds, the subject's assertion of himself within a system of relations embodying rules and expectations is real and 'eternal': an irreducible mode of existence of the human being.

In Althusser's somewhat manichean version of the traditional Marxist ideology critique, while *all* ideology (class and classless) embodies imaginary, i.e. non-scientific, relations to the world, ideology in a class society also has the function of masking from the individual his total lack of autonomy, allowing him falsely to present himself as 'a subject with consciousness' with 'ideas which he has freely chosen in full consciousness'.[21] While Althusser's central thought, that subjectivity is an irreducible mode of human existence, is correct, this manichean application is not. Members and representatives of the working class are not necessarily victims of ideological mystification in adopting the internal point of view towards certain constitutional arrangements of a bourgeois state;[22] still less are they such victims in adopting it towards the day-to-day operation of the law, both civil and criminal.

The traditional Marxist ideology critique helps us to locate the internal point of view in a more material context, but, at least in its Althusserian-manichean form, it gives little guidance as to how we should integrate it into our picture of the *Rechtsstaat*. Traditional legal ideology told us that a legal order connected legally free, legally equal legal subjects; traditional Marxist ideology critique told us that that picture was a deception masking substantive inequalities between parties and substantive unfreedoms constraining action. The unspoken implication was that, with the withering-away of the superstructures, the content of that ideology too would wither-away. The mythological nature of that version of the withering-away thesis has already been discussed. My position, in contrast, is that, in the passage from the actual legal order, embodying and sometimes masking gross structural inequalities, to an envisaged legal order, embodying different social relations, conceptions of rights and legal subjectivity neither disappear nor are transcended in an *Aufhebung*, but are internalized and applied concretely by the agents of change.

Habermas

In trying to envisage this rather complex process, we have to consider both the forms of possible communication between human beings and the forms of relations within which such communication can take place. Here Habermas's reflections on communication are important for our problem. Habermas has distinguished such forms as transmitting orders, asserting rights, making agreements and commitments. For these forms to be successfully carried out, without 'distortion', different kinds of relationship are required between the communicating parties. Applying this idea to the practices of the *Rechtsstaat*, based on the assertion and defence of rights, we can say that the parties should have some measure of equal access to power, otherwise the practices remain an empty charade, the abstraction of legal *Indifferenz* of Marx's *Grundrisse*. Habermas envisaged consensus as the goal of all communication: the reaching of agreement via the rational procedures of argumentation. He distinguished different procedures appropriate to different domains, from the deductive formalization of logic and mathematics to the relatively informal (but nonetheless rational) rules of practical reasoning designed to reach agreed decisions in practical matters, personal, social and political. In the envisaged 'ideal speech situation', relatively egalitarian social relations between free individuals would together guarantee the possibility of consensus. Thus for the consensus to be genuine, all parties to it must be free to express their opinions without the constraints of relations of domination/subordination.[23]

Of the many problems raised by Habermas's communications theory one is particularly relevant to jurisprudence: the nature of the consensus itself. The idea that the goal of all communication is consensus is not without ambiguity when applied to the law. For if the rational order is one in which all would agree (within the proper context of social relations and rules of argument) on all questions of policy, then there is a danger that the model will yield uncomfortably totalitarian conclusions: the union of reason and norm, in which there are no irreducible differences in outlook, impervious to rational discussion, seems to condemn those who disagree with the rational consensus to a political limbo (occupied, of course, by those failing to participate in the exercise of the general will in the *Social Contract*). Assuming that 'consensus' is not to be understood in that totalitarian way, then all that is implied is that ground rules can be established and agreed more or less consensually which would allow all kinds of substantive disagreements concerning desirable 'experiments of living' to coexist within legal limits. That more relativist position, derived from Mill, has been advocated throughout this book, though it is not evidently compatible with Habermas's high rationalism.

With these reservations, we can draw an important lesson from Habermas's communications theory, that the conditions of genuine subjectivity and the conditions of political democracy are inseparable. A legal order is an order connecting legal subjects; to be a legal subject in the full sense, a person must be able to assert his rights as *his* rights, his constitutional rights as rights stemming from *his* constitution. In this sense, the operation of the *Rechtsstaat* in a form which is not just a legal charade demands that a consensus in the relativist (Millian) sense is reached and that consensus is attainable only through a transformation of power relations. To illustrate the point by a comparison with games: in making *my* move, *my* bid, etc. I assume that my opponent is not cheating and that the game as a whole is not rigged (as in playing the fruit machines). In so far as the positive legal system corresponds to the fruit machine, the internal point of view is indeed a deception, but the counter-goal of the genuine *Rechtsstaat* is not thereby devalued.

6.3 THE LAW AND THE *RECHTSSTAAT*

Our reflections on despotism in Mill, on legitimacy in Hart and on the conditions for realizing legitimacy in the Marxist ideology critics have led us to draw a distinction between the existence of a legal system and the existence of what Hart would call a 'society with law' or, in our terminology, a *Rechtsstaat*.[24] We have seen that formal criteria for the existence of a *Rechsstaat* are not readily available and that a particular society may correspond more or less closely to the model, elements of which have been sketched in previous chapters. In the present section these elements will be assembled in a rather more ordered fashion and we shall consider ways in which different societies may fail to embody one or more of those elements.

Stated dogmatically, the *Rechtsstaat* can be defined as a society ruled by procedural justice and guaranteeing the universal and equal distribution of basic constitutional rights to all citizens.

(1) *Procedural justice*

The regularity, predictability and reliability of the administration of the law is an essential component of the *Rechtsstaat*: a virtue, that of procedural justice, for its proponents; a vice, that of abstraction for its critics. In considering Unger's critique of formalism in chapter 1, we saw that at the heart of procedural justice is Hart's principle of 'treating like cases alike' and that that principle is not essentially connected with the vice of abstraction-formalism, in so far as it leaves open to political-social decision the question of criteria of likeness/unlikeness of cases.[25]

The question of procedural justice entered into the positivism/natural law controversy concerning the status of law during the Nazi period in Germany, in the famous debate between Hart and Fuller in 1958.[26] Against what he took to be Hart's positivist thesis that law represents order simpliciter and that in so far as the Nazi regime imposed order it embodied law, Fuller argued that:[27]

> Law, considered merely as order, contains . . . its own implicit morality. This morality of order must be respected if we are to create anything that can be called law, even bad law.

The presence or absence, or, in the case of Nazism, the survival of annihilation, of the *Rechtsstaat* 'is always a matter of degree . . . We have . . . to inquire how much of a legal system survived the general debasement and perversion of all forms of social order'.[28] Fuller instanced three characteristic forms of Nazi order: retroactive statutes, secret enactments and the 'bypassing' of inconvenient legal forms so as to 'act through the party in the streets'. In his outstanding chapter 'The Spirit of National Socialist Law' in *Hitler: The Führer and the People,*[29] Stern illustrated these three irregularities with many more examples and added three further forms of the destruction of procedural justice: subordination of regular sentencing to policy directives,[30] the destruction of courtroom procedure, so that acquittals resulted not in the defendant's release but in his being handed over to the Gestapo[31] and the release of agents of the state, in particular the Gestapo, from all legal answerability with respect to arrest, interrogation and detention.[32] Under the Nazi regime the law became[33]

> . . . the exercise of objective-seeming power in support of purely arbitrary and subjective decisions, its true character in no way hidden but emphasized by the mock-formality of its wordings.

The Nazi regime, then, represents the clearest exemplar of the destruction of the *Rechtsstaat* at the level of procedural justice, the regular, systematic procedure of treating like cases alike. The experience of the Nazi period has shown that when the law is isolated from democratic political endorsement and also from the other components of the *Rechtsstaat* to be considered below, it becomes abstract and formalistic in the pejorative sense: fragile and open to subversion for instrumental policy goals.[34] Procedural justice is an essential component of the *Rechtsstaat*: without it no constitutional rights are safe. But it is a necessary, not a sufficient, condition for the existence of the *Rechtsstaat*. To illustrate this, we shall distinguish two other forms which fall short of the *Rechtsstaat*, even where their procedures may be impeccably regular: that in which rights are formal, not real (2); that in which rights are unequally distributed among sections of the population (3).

(2) *Basic constitutional rights only formal*

A society may embody procedural justice (regularity and predictability in the enforcement of its regulations), yet still fail to be a *Rechtsstaat*, in the sense that it does not define and enforce citizens' basic constitutional rights. The combination of definition, on the one hand, and enforceability, on the other, is important, in view of the two ways in which citizens' rights may be vulnerable: from the informality of common law systems[35] and from the abstraction of formally constitutional orders where the means of enforcing rights are not available.[36] The distinction between (1) and (2) is a real one. Questions concerning the regularity of the administration of rules are formally independent of questions concerning the distribution of rights and duties. But, though formally independent, they are, in political reality, closely linked. It is no accident that the French Declaration of the Rights of Man and the Citizen demanded both the right of political participation for citizens, answerability on the part of government agents, and the end of arbitrary procedures. For without a system of enforceable rights, the maintenance of procedural justice remains dependent on the good will of those in power. The tendency towards irregularity and arbitrariness is inscribed within all non-democratic forms of government. Nazi Germany was the paradigm case of the destruction of both (1) and (2). Cases where (1) is preserved in the day-to-day conduct of citizens' lives, but where constitutionally inscribed rights are in fact hollow or fictive, include the socialist countries with respect to many elementary political and cultural freedoms, such as those formally guaranteed by Article 50 of the Soviet Constitution: 'freedom of speech, of the press and of assembly, meetings, street processions and demonstrations'.[37] For institutional reasons, those forms of political organization leave particularly little space for either the assertion of cultural pluralism or the exertion of citizens' control on the wielders of political power. In contrast, the forms and instruments for defending civil liberties have been more or less successfully attained and preserved in some of the capitalist countries. But from that premiss it does not follow that their defence is ever secure against subversion and recuperation by the agents of power in those countries.

(3) *Basic constitutional rights unequally distributed*

For Hart, a paradigm case of a complex, advanced and procedurally regular legal system enforcing morally obnoxious laws would be that of South Africa. Mentioned sometimes directly, sometimes obliquely, the model of South Africa haunts the discussions of law, morality and justice in *The Concept of Law*:[38]

> . . . it is plain that neither the law nor the accepted morality of societies need extend their minimal protections and benefits to all within their scope, and often they have not done so. In slave-owning societies the sense that the slaves are human beings, not mere objects to be used, may be lost by the dominant group, who may yet remain morally sensitive to each other's claims and interests. . . . Nazi Germany and South Africa offer parallels unpleasantly near to us in time. . .
>
> No doubt the contention that a legal system must treat all human beings within its scope as entitled to certain basic protections and freedoms, is now generally accepted as a statement of an ideal of obvious relevance in the criticism of law. . .
>
> [But] municipal legal systems, with their characteristic structure of primary and secondary rules, have long endured though they have flouted these principles of justice.

Here, once again, I should want to accept Hart's positivist programme of distinguishing questions concerning the existence conditions of a legal system from questions concerning the morality of that system. But, once again, I should want to shift the focus of our attention from that dichotomy to the question left on the margin of Hart's schema: whether or not a given society embodies a *Rechtsstaat*.

In examining that question, we can admit a little more detail concerning the South African system into our reflections than Hart does into his.

The institutionalized racial exploitation of the apartheid system is expressed at each level of the legal system. At the level of constitutional provisions, non-Europeans are effectively excluded from political power and responsibility. At the level of the criminal law, their freedom of action is circumscribed by laws specifically applicable to them and not to Europeans. At the level of private law, they are excluded from functioning as legal subjects in all areas giving access to economic power: contract, property, etc. At this third level it could be argued that South Africa does not constitute a unified *Rechtsstaat*, even a deformed one, at all. Sections of the non-European population[39] have been subject to a 'Native' Code, which has consigned the black woman governed by the Code to being 'a perpetual minor in law', deprived of independent legal powers[40] and has channelled the black man's contractual powers through his traditional village or kraal head.[41] The tendency towards the disintegration of the unity of even the formal *Rechtsstaat* is reinforced by the present black 'homelands' policy: a fragmentation designed to enforce racial supremacy rather than pluralism.

It is also problematic whether procedural justice can, in reality, survive in such an inegalitarian climate, where only a racial minority have effective access to the means of enforcing constitutional rights through the courts. The literature concerning these irregularities is massive and detailed.[42]

(4) *Two conditions for the existence of the* Rechtsstaat

Though it is not possible to find formal criteria for the existence of a *Rechtsstaat*, in terms of necessary and sufficient conditions, since its realization is always a matter of degree, we can still define the *Rechtsstaat* more or less formally, as we have done above, as a society ruled by procedural justice and guaranteeing the universal and equal distribution of basic constitutional rights to all citizens. Our previous reflections on (2) and (3) lead us to conclude that both those components are more or less dependent on two factors: (a) a degree of egalitarianism which makes the assertion of rights a reality, not a formality (Rousseau's condition); (b) a degree of independence for the judiciary *vis-à-vis* the government which allows for it genuinely to adjudicate concerning assertions of citizens' rights, particularly against government agencies (Locke's condition).

(a) *Rousseau's condition*

. . . by equality, we should understand, not that the degrees of power and riches are to be absolutely identical for everybody; but that power shall never be great enough for violence, and shall always be exercised by virtue of rank and law; and that, in respect of riches, no citizen shall every be wealthy enough to buy another, and none poor enough to be forced to sell himself.[43]

Marxist critics have stressed the abstraction and formality of rights under capitalism when Rousseau's condition is not fulfilled. In a nutshell:[44]

. . . though wealthy and poor are equally entitled to a fair trial, are 'equal before the law', the wealthy have access to better legal counsel, have more opportunity to influence the administration of justice both in specific cases and in determining what crimes will be prosecuted, and have greater ability to secure laws that favor their interests.

I differ from the Marxist critics only where they refuse to carry Rousseau's insight into the interconnection between rights and egalitarianism through into their vision of communism and where they fail to connect the struggle for a redistribution of power in high-technology capitalism with the struggle for constitutionally guaranteed civil rights.

(b) *Locke's condition*

. . . it is unreasonable for Men to be Judges in their own cases, since Self-love will make Men partial to themselves and their Friends.[45]

Locke's advocacy, on grounds of fairness, of a division of powers, of the institution of an impartial judge or 'umpire', became an important component of the liberal political ideology of the eighteenth century, culminating in the United States Constitution. In Dworkin's epigram, 'Our constitutional system rests on a particular moral theory, namely that men have moral rights against the state'.[46] In order that that theory should be realized, some real distance must be established in terms of rights and duties between government agents, on the one hand, and agents of the judiciary, on the other. Once again, we are faced with a question of degree, concerning the extent to which that distance is established in different systems. Here we can distinguish questions of constitutional powers (judicial review of the constitutionality of legislation, citizens' rights to sue government agencies, etc.) from questions of organization of the legal profession (recruitment and appointment of judges, relationship of advocates to their clients, conditions of payment, promotion, etc.).[47] In both these respects Locke's condition can be more or less successfully realized.

Radical critics of the law in capitalist countries either stress the unreality of the separation of powers, which is seen as a sham, a cosmetic dressing for a particular function of the state, or, recognizing that the judiciary does have a certain autonomy, are critical of that very autonomy, as an obstacle to radical political change. It is not surprising that the former criticism is more prevalent in the United Kingdom, the latter in the United States, given the different constitutional developments of the two countries.[48]

But, before considering those criticisms, I would stress the importance of maintaining a comparative perspective on the topic. From the standpoint of a system in which judicial autonomy has been reduced almost to vanishing point, but in which political developments make it once again a possibility, that autonomy is seen as playing a vital role in altering the balance of power between citizens and government. The most striking recent example was Poland in 1980–1, where the Supreme Court 'upheld an appeal by the Solidarity free trade union against amendments to its statutes imposed by a lower court'.[49] The significance of this case, in the East European context of widespread conflation between government and party functions, was that the Supreme Court overruled a judgement in favour of the party: 'The Union had appealed to the court principally to delete a clause written into its statutes by the Warsaw District Court . . . acknowledging the supremacy of the Communist Party'. In pronouncing both that the lower court 'had overstepped its competence' and that Solidarity's 'original statutes . . . conformed to the Polish constitution', the Polish Supreme Court was fulfilling a central function of an independent judiciary. An important aim of Solidarity's struggle was to go further and to free lower courts too from their dependence on the party apparatus and to endow them with some real autonomy.[50] Along with the other achievements of those years, this attempt was to fall victim to martial law.

The critique of the 'myth' of the autonomy of the judiciary in the United Kingdom has been most systematically pursued by John Griffith, for whom[51]

> Her Majesty's judges are an essential part of the government of the country. And the fact that they may, as part of their duties, sometimes protect the individual from the arbitrary behaviour of other public officials does not make this less so. . . . they are concerned to uphold the system of government, to preserve law and order, to avoid economic and political disturbance on a national scale, to help run the Western parliamentary democratic capitalist constitution which puts them where they are and maintains them in authority.

He finds ready confirmation for that view in Lord Devlin's denial of

> . . . the validity of the constitutional theory that the judiciary is the neutral force between government and governed: 'British judges have never practised such detachment . . . In the criminal law the judges regard themselves as at least as much concerned as the executive with the preservation of law and order'.

Griffith's book, *The Politics of the Judiciary*, is an extended polemical essay on the sociology of the legal system, designed to demonstrate the essential unity of the juridico-political establishment:[52]

> The community of rulers is a close and narrow community. Judges and politicians do not have to agree on the details of policies, they do not have to belong to the same political party. There is no conspiracy

because there is no need for a conspiracy. All share the same fundamental premises.

In his normative conclusions, Griffith is almost wholly pessimistic about the capacity of the judiciary in Britain ever to play a genuinely autonomous role as it does in the USA.[53] He sees the British judiciary, because of its method of recruitment, as consistently hostile to progressive judicial activism like that of the US Supreme Court. This temperamental hostility, deriving from its professional formation, is reinforced by the relatively informal division of powers between government and judiciary, the 'ultimate, if partial, subservience of the judiciary to the government',[54] and the absence of a written constitution and constitutional Court. Griffith's pessimism extends to the movement to introduce a Bill of Rights in this country, possibly by the entrenchment of the European Convention on Human Rights.[55] The detailed history of this movement during the 1970s and early 1980s lies outside my concerns, but, as I have noted already, it would be wrong to underestimate the role of the European Court of Human Rights as an agent for enforcing the minimal standards of the *Rechtsstaat* on unwilling British governments and judiciaries, or the role of the EEC Court in highlighting the inadequacies of domestic social legislation. Griffith concludes:[56]

> It is difficult to see how the welfare of the individual would be promoted by the enactment of such provisions [as the European Convention on Human Rights] if they were to be interpreted by the judiciary of today.

That conclusion may be too pessimistic for this reason: successive British governments have made the political decision that adherence to these European Conventions is the necessary (if unwelcome) price that has to be paid for deriving political and economic benefits from European institutions. The recalcitrance of the British judiciary has been, to some extent at least, overridden by political necessity.

How far that healthy tendency can be extended is an open question. But there has been widespread debate[57] on the possible ways of incorporating a new Bill of Rights by entrenching the European Convention of Human Rights in some effective way into British law, ranging from Lord Scarman's most radical proposals to set up a Supreme Court with constitutional powers equal to the United States one through to the more modest compromise proposals of Lord Wade and others. This debate suggests that the British judiciary is not so universally philistine and subservient as Griffith suggests and that even its most stubborn opponents may be forced to submit to the more advanced standards of the European *Rechtsstaat*.

The central question raised for us by this debate concerns the direction of rational political activity. If Marx and Griffith (in his more unguarded moments) are correct, if autonomy is and never can be more than a hypocritical sham, then there is little point in struggling to make it reality. I reject that element of the Marxist legacy and hold that the degree of autonomy attained by the judiciary of a given state or association of states is itself a function of the political sophistication of that state or states and can be altered by the active participation of its citizens in the political process.

In perhaps no other country in the world are the citizens so imbued with the ideology of constitutionalism as in the USA. The Constitution is taught to American schoolchildren as a way both of instilling a sense of national identity and of forming a set of relatively active, participatory attitudes towards the law as an expression of fundamental human rights.[58] The United States Constitution defines the greatest space within which citizens can challenge government agencies through the courts, even if, through its combination of technological expertise and condensation of executive power, it raises the stakes in that challenge increasingly high.[59] The political system embodied in the US Constitution, is extremely complex. It balances extreme devolution of power to the states on the one hand, and residual federal power, on the other, and at the same time balances the three 'branches of government', legislative, executive and judicial. Thus the US judiciary is called upon to adjudicate on a wide range of questions many of which would elsewhere not be subject to judicial review. The Supreme Court is the highest constitutional court both on the constitutionality of state and federal legislation and on the relative powers of the executive and legislative branches. The Supreme Court's changing attitudes over the years, swinging between the poles of more or less passive endorsement ('judicial restraint') and a more critical, interventionist stance ('judicial activism') have been well charted and analysed by Dworkin.[60] The moral of that history is that the existence of an institutionally independent judiciary does not, in itself, guarantee that that institution will be used critically and effectively in the protection of rights. For it to do so, a political will is required. But it does show the value of such an institution both in defining the constitutional machinery and in widening citizens' expectations about the 'limits of the possible' concerning the *Rechtsstaat*.

According to Nonet and Selznick the positive contribution of 'autonomous law', characterized by the separation of powers, was that it brought constraints on the exercise of power by officials and that it raised 'expectations regarding consistency and fairness of official action';[61] its negative feature, for them, was its 'rule-centredness', its alliance with the orderly values of the bureaucracy, its promotion of regular procedure over substantive justice and its conservative tendency to support 'law and order'.[62] I have already criticized other aspects of Nonet's and Selznick's account in chapter 1. Here I would simply reiterate the thought that if legal autonomy is understood in institutional terms as entailing an independent judiciary and in procedural terms as entailing regularity, reliability and fairness, then it in no way needs to be allied to conservative political positions. Where Nonet and Selznick saw the development of successful 'social advocacy' as a move away from judicial autonomy (in the direction of so-called 'responsive law') I should prefer to follow Dworkin's lead in seeing it as a strengthening of the independent force of the judiciary through 'judicial activism'. Nonet's and Selznick's typology has the curious consequence that legal 'autonomy' is associated with judicial 'restraint', or, in more brutal terms, subservience.

It is interesting that British socialists, while critical of the lack of genuine autonomy of the British judiciary, have from the beginning been equally suspicious of the European Convention of Human Rights:[63]

In Britain the Labour party was in power and, not seeing the emergence of a European federation of socialist States, was suspicious of the Conservative party's enthusiastic support of the European idea. . . . hoping to control affairs at home through a reactionary federated Europe.

Patricia Hewitt sees that suspicion as still justified:[64]

Socialists are right to fear that the increased power conferred on the courts by a new Bill of Rights would be used to strike down, for instance, a wealth tax or a nationalization statute as contrary to the 'peaceful enjoyment of possessions' guaranteed to individuals *and* to corporations by Protocol 1 of the Convention.

on the grounds that:

Interference with private property is indeed permitted by the Convention 'in accordance with law' and 'in the public interest', but the courts are scarcely the appropriate judges of what economic policies should be pursued in the public interest.

That fear has proved groundless. Article 1 of the First Protocol of the Convention does indeed state that:[65]

Every natural or legal person is entitled to the peaceful enjoyment of his possessions. No one shall be deprived of his possessions except in the public interest and subject to the conditions provided for by law and by the general principles of international law.

The preceding provisions shall not, however, in any way impair the right of the State to enforce such laws as it deems necessary to control the use of property in accordance with the general interest or to secure the payment of taxes or other contributions or penalties.

Interpreting the reference to 'the public interest' broadly, the Commission has rejected the majority of cases brought under Article 1 of the Protocol . . . 'as instances where deprivation or control [by the State] is necessary'.[66] In contrast, the 'activist' role of the Commission and Court in protecting civil liberties against authoritative infringement by governments, with respect to fair trial, detainees' and prisoners' rights, police surveillance, etc. has been wholly progressive and has encountered opposition from successive British governments, both Tory and Labour. Indeed, as Beddard points out, 'The Conservative Party's attitude when again achieving office showed very little difference . . . from that of Labour!' The Council of Europe's Data Protection Convention may be hoped to fulfil a similar function in forcing the governments of signatory states to comply with more stringent controls than they would spontaneously impose on themselves, particularly when such regulations are backed by 'the pressing need of multinational corporations and governments themselves to be able to transfer computerised data across national boundaries'.[67]

To conclude, Locke's condition is as essential as Rousseau's. Governments and their agencies should not be judges in their own causes. Judicial autonomy is not the natural enemy of socialism and the antipathy of British socialists to the imposition of supra-national norms, if it is not due to simple chauvinism, is due to the pervasive influence of different confused tendencies of the Marxist heritage, which condense into a general antipathy to the law, the judiciary and the formalized, necessarily artificial style of legal argumentation. Against that tradition, I assert that, in an advanced technological society, power can be more equally distributed among citizens only within a system of complex and specific individual and corporate rights, whose recognition and protection requires an 'activist' and autonomous judiciary.[68] Given the distance between that ideal and the reality of the contemporary British judicial system, British adherence to more advanced European institutions can change the situation only for the better.[69]

6.4. SUBSTANTIVE RIGHTS

The *Rechtsstaat*, it has been maintained, is the only form of effective protection of the integrity of individuals and groups within an advanced technological society, even if an elaborate system of rights, duties and division of powers may be unnecessary in simpler societies. Why should that be?

Many years ago John Plamenatz issued a challenge to

Engels's particular variant of the withering-away thesis. Engels, he maintained:[70]

> . . . took it for granted that, if states were first created by privileged classes, and if there had never been a state that did not enable some class to exploit another, it followed that there would be no need for a state where there was no class exploitation. It needs only a moment's thought to see that this assumption is groundless. Neither Engels nor any other Marxist has ever produced good reasons for believing that, in any except the most primitive society, there would, if there were no classes, be no need for a state – that is, for the services of a special hierarchy of persons maintaining order, if necessary by force.

After attempting for many years to rebut it, I should now want to accept the correctness of Plamenatz's challenge, envisaging, schematically, the following possibilities for a society which has reached an advanced stage of technological sophistication and social diversity:

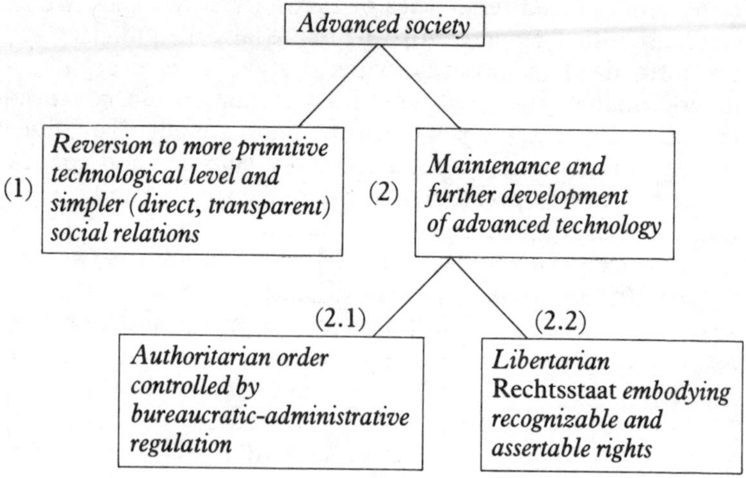

Figure 6.1. A Realistic Reply to Plamenatz's Challenge.

I have suggested already that Marx's own thesis of the primacy of the productive forces, in its modest, defensible form, isolated from the *Gemeinschaft* nostalgia with which it is tainted, entails simply that complex technology demands a complex division of labour to operate it: increasingly specialized functions of accountancy and management alongside the equally specialized technical functions. An equally modest version of Marxist historicism suggests that rational human beings will choose option (2) over option (1), though it denies that that choice is inevitable, universal or made without heavy social cost in terms of lost values.

The complex division of labour demanded by (2) inevitably distributes power unequally and irrationally unless the use made of that power is rigorously controlled within a system of rules. In order that the system of rules should be fairly and impartially enforced, thus corresponding to Locke's condition, and in order that it should be sufficiently specific in content and application, so as to correspond to the complexity of the given technology, the division of powers conferring both expertise and autonomy on at least two separate 'branches' of administration (the legislature on the one hand and the judiciary on the other) cannot be expected to wither-away, although it can be subverted by authoritarian reaction.

Applying that thought to the new industrial era inaugurated by the revolution in information technology, we can locate power in advanced societies, both capitalist and socialist, in access to information and the use that can be made of that information by individuals and groups. Thus an authoritarian regime (2.1.) insures a monopoly of important information concerning private citizens in government hands and blocks any moves towards equalizing access to stored information concerning policy options. Characteristic of bureaucratic-administrative regulation in the socialist countries, this combination of unregulated surveillance and secrecy by governments is also present, to different degrees, in capitalist countries at a low level of constitutional development, particularly the United Kingdom.[71]

The central task for the law in a libertarian regime (2.2.), from our perspective, is to mediate between the technological–rational imperative of maintaining and developing the productive forces (in this case the forces of information technology) and the moral imperative of defending individuals' and groups' increasingly fragile rights against their misuse. The immense literature on the problems of controlling this new technology within the law, in particular the new menaces raised by it to civil liberties, lies outside the scope of this book.[72] I allude simply to two important problems raised by it: the problem of privacy and the problem of freedom of information.

Privacy

Privacy is important, but also vulnerable, in advanced societies in so far as it constitutes the core of certain traditional liberal-constitutional freedoms and in so far as the extent to which the assertion and maintenance of those freedoms itself determines the balance of power between citizens and government.

For many years lawyers in the United States have been attempting to refine Judge Cooley's 'right to be let alone'[73] into a legally applicable right to privacy. The Federal Privacy Act of 1974 'regulates the [collection and] transfer of personal information by federal government agencies', it 'covers both manual and automatically processed records'; it 'gives individuals the right to see and correct records kept on them by federal government agencies'.[74] The United States Act has concentrated on government, rather than on corporate, data collection and transmission,[75] but in that domain it has sought to give some degree of statutory protection to two traditional liberal-constitutional freedoms, freedom of ideas and freedom of association.[76] While the Act's effectiveness as an instrument of protection has not yet been fully tested,[77] its presence on the statute book highlights the distance which the United Kingdom lags behind the United States in this respect. In Patricia Hewitt's summary judgement: 'The citizen of the United Kingdom is completely unprotected by law against the collection and use of personal information.'[78]

Freedom of Information

Comparative studies substantiate the view that the United Kingdom is 'one of the most secret countries of the western world'.[79] The Official Secrets Act is merely the most notorious example of the battery of formal and informal powers available to British governments to prevent historians, trade-unionists and ordinary citizens from gaining access to the vast store of information in official hands. As with privacy, so with open government, the left in the past in this country has been tempted by the thought that the law is a necessarily ineffective weapon given the present balance of power between the classes: that campaigning for legislation on these issues is a luxury for liberal pressure groups, but more or less irrelevant to the central issue of the class struggle. While that attitude has changed in recent years, pressure for more open government has been successfully deflected.

In countries corresponding more closely to the model of the *Rechtsstaat*, in particular in the United States and in Scandinavia, but also elsewhere in Western Europe, the citizen has some legal protection of his freedom 'to receive and impart information'; in addition, his '"right to know" implies that there is a corresponding obligation. If there is a right to know about government, then government has a duty to inform.'[80] Once again, to make this right a reality, both Rousseau's condition and Locke's condition must be more or less fulfilled: access to officially stored information must be guaranteed equally to all citizens and a relatively neutral arbitrator (the Federal Courts in the United States, the Ombudsman in Sweden)[81] must be empowered to arbitrate between officials and citizens.

Freedom of Information vs. Privacy?

Writing two years after the passing of the US Freedom of Information Act and five years before the passing of the Privacy Act, Miller was pessimistic about the erosion of personal privacy which the former Act would bring about:[82]

> The conflict between the public's right to know and the individual's right to have some control over the flow of personal information held by the Government is extremely difficult to resolve, and it is doubtful that new legislation . . . could offer more than general guidelines for handling the kaleidoscopic factual problems that will arise.
>
> In essence, it [the Freedom of Information Act] reverses the

traditional presumption in favor of personal privacy, and places the burden on the information holding agency to find a specific statutory ground for refusing to honor a request for disclosure.

Until the Privacy Act has been more fully tested it will not be clear whether that pessimism is justified. But the conflict between the principles embodied in the two Acts could in principle and, it would seem, in practice too, be resolved by systematically distinguishing between natural persons on the one hand and corporate or legal persons on the other, so that the privacy of the former and the openness of the latter could be promoted together.[83] In view of the complex array of roles a citizen can play in an advanced society and the impossibility of drawing absolute lines between public and private domains, the possibility of conflict between the two principles cannot be excluded: investigation into the properly public actions and deliberations of individuals as office-holders may unintendedly reveal facts about those same individuals as private citizens. But there seems to be no reason of principle why such conflicts should be particularly resistant to properly drafted legislation.[84]

Foundations?

Both privacy and freedom of information are valued in advanced societies in so far as they are component parts of a particular form of life, that of pluralism. In it, individuals and groups exercise a degree of autonomy and control over the conditions of their existence and their 'experiments of living' are more or less effectively protected within the coercive framework of the *Rechtsstaat*. In Miller's succinct summary:[85]

> . . . the basic attribute of an effective right to privacy is the individual's ability to control the flow of information concerning or describing him – a capability that often is essential to the establishment of social relationships and the maintenance of personal freedom. Correlatively, when the individual is deprived of control over the information spigot, he in some measure becomes subservient to those people and institutions that are able to gain acess to it.

Fried deepened this account of privacy as a component of liberal pluralism by showing that one's very identity as a person depends on the maintenance of a degree of privacy since the negation of privacy is the negation of 'respect, love, friendship and trust'.[86] This, Fried maintained, is for two reasons: first, that the domain of the private constitutes for the individual a moral capital, which he can properly transmit to the loved one and deny to the public;[87] second, that individuals must maintain their 'integrity as persons' in order to be able to engage in those personal relations at all. Now what constitutes both 'moral capital' and 'integrity as persons' will vary from society to society: and much of it will be mediated through symbolic forms like eating, excreting, etc.[88] But it is arguable that the presence of some area or areas of privacy is a universal phenomenon, that everywhere there are some marks which constitute the person as a person, that stripping him of those marks strips him of personhood.[89]

I would differ from Fried only in emphasis. I prefer to connect privacy more directly with power relations in society, so that the limits of the private are the limits within which individuals can engage in these valued forms of social relations and retain the psychological and moral capital to do so, but within which they can also retreat from such relationships since, within a pluralist framework, the right to privacy must also be defended for the unloving and untrustworthy. As Mill emphasized in *On Liberty,* social freedom entails freedom to make mistakes, even fundamental mistakes concerning forms of life.

Equally, the citizen's 'right to know', could be founded on an 'exceptionless or absolute human claim right', in Finnis's formulation, namely:[90]

> . . . the right not to be positively lied to in any situation (e.g. teaching, preaching, research publication, news broadcasting) in which factual communication (as distinct from fiction, jest, or poetry) is reasonably expected.

Now, truth-telling may be a virtue and lying a vice at all levels of human life. It may even be a presupposition of social life that any individual may normally expect to be told the truth by his neighbour who, in turn, is under a general moral obligation not intentionally to mislead him. But until individuals are inserted in particular social roles relative to one another, the stronger obligations entailed by freedom of information laws, embodying both the citizen's right to know and the government's duty actively to enforce disclosure, simply do not apply to them. Thus the aspiration to freedom of information goes beyond Finnis's minimal 'right not to be positively lied to'[91] in so far as it includes more extensive rights and duties, but at the same time it operates within a relatively restricted context, that of socially ordered power. It establishes rights and duties within an arena of responsibilities and penalties for failure to fulfill them, defining more or less formally the limits of legitimate activity for agents of political and economic power.

The aspirations both to privacy and to freedom of information at the legal-political level are thus continuous with aspirations at other levels of human existence, but not, on my presentation, derivable therefrom. Those values are asserted and defended at the legal-political level as distinct rights and duties because, in an advanced technological society, there is no other way of marking out a space at that level where Millian autonomy and pluralism may flourish.

6.5 DEGREES OF RELATIVISM

I conclude by assessing the limits of the relativism to which I am committed in my account of the *Rechtsstaat*. Relativism in moral and political matters involves a scepticism concerning the limits of reason as arbitrator between particular values and between whole value systems, concerning the limits of cross-cultural communication and concerning the ontological grounding of value systems. It would be a rash author who would embark on a reconstruction of the whole of moral philosophy and metaphysics in the *envoi* to a polemical essay in jurisprudence and such a reconstruction would be necessary for an adequate defence of the relativism hinted at in the book and summarized in the previous sentence. Rather than attempt such a reconstruction, I simply draw together the relativist threads and leave the reader to unpick the tattered fabric they compose.

Real and utopian models

For a particular, historically determined society in process of change there is a range of possible models of development available. Given the power of the human imagination, the range of imaginary, utopian models goes beyond that of real (available) models.[92] The range of real models is limited by what may be termed material constraints, on the one hand, and phenomenological constraints, on the other, which interact to lay down the horizon of possible social outcomes.

By material constraints I refer to the relations of compatibility/incompatibility outlined by Marx in the base/superstructure model.[93] Given a certain technological level, only a limited number of organizational and normative forms are compatible with its maintenance, reproduction and development. As we saw in the last section, the consistent advocate of a return to simpler forms of life may indeed seek to dismantle the technical base of the advanced society which he criticizes. But, in the absence of such dismantling, the nostalgic model of radically simplified social relations is not a real model. The only real models are variants on the spectrum between bureaucratic-administrative regulation and the *Rechtsstaat.*

Utopianism in this context is the idea that it is possible to combine two incompatible elements: high technology in the productive system with simple transparent relations in the superstructure. But why should utopianism of this kind be dangerous? Only for this reason: that by drawing attention towards an unreal model, it also diverts attention from a real model, that of the authoritarian bureaucratic-administrative regulation.

Parallel to the material constraints on aspirations to return to simplicity there are phenomenological constraints, by which I mean the limits imposed by their experiences and resultant levels of consciousness on the range of forms of life available to people at different stages of development. Certain 'alternative' groups within advanced societies seek to reconstruct simpler, communitarian forms of life through the explicit negation of undesirable features of those societies. But just in so far as it is a reconstruction, it would seem to be impossible to live a reconstruction of a traditional form of life in the same way as that form of life would be lived prior to its transformation.[94] As Charles Taylor has pointed out, a form of life wholly infused by symbolic, expressive, ritual categories cannot be reconstructed after the systematic retreat of those categories from domains conquered by the categories of the natural sciences even by an individual whose aim is once again 'to combine the two in our civilization'.[95] More specifically, there are constraints imposed on the range of possible forms of life by available knowledge. The sciences of biology and sociology between them have made any 'natural', unreflective acceptance of racist and sexist assumptions in our societies impossible, though they have, of course, made possible new and more highly wrought versions of those attitudes.[96]

Choosing between forms of life

What sense does it make to talk of 'choosing' between whole forms of life? Can there be any rational choice between radically different orderings of value systems, such that the very criteria of choice are put in question by opting for one or the other? Imagine a more or less closed society in which social integration is a prime value and in which an individual gains honour by promoting the interests of his kinsmen in certain socially approved forms. In that society, the values of the *Rechtsstaat,* particularly individual freedom and equality before the law and assertable rights and duties, might scarcely feature. For a 'choice' between the two forms of life to be a rational one, there would need to be some continuity of criteria, some 'common currency',[97] in Bernard Williams's terminology, in terms of which the models could be assessed. But that continuity is just what is broken in major social transformations.

Nonetheless, a major social transformation can take place, guided by some degree of rational agency, during which the component values of a society's value system are reordered, sometimes radically. Agents of that process also seem capable of assessing the cost of the transition *ex post facto* in ways that suggest that the 'common currency' metaphor is partly misleading. The process may be better understood in terms of a *Gestalt* reordering of figure and ground, so that values dominant and subordinate in the old forms of life change position in the new one.[98] *Gemeinschaftlich* values may be eclipsed in a process of modernization, but they do not necessarily disappear. They can be recalled and revitalized in communities within the new order and provide a reservoir of experience for imaginative comparison between the lost order and the new one.

In jurisprudence, John Finnis has recently employed a similar *Gestaltist* approach to the problem of understanding the ways in which value systems are reordered, but his philosophical anthropology is explicitly objectivist and naturalistic, in contrast to mine. For Finnis, the '*outlines of the common good*' are discernible by 'practical reason' (p. 214).[99] one's 'own intelligent grasp of the indemonstrable (because self-evident) first principles of [one's] own practical reasoning', broadened by historical and anthropological reflection (p. 85). He is also explicitly non-reductionist, asserting that the seven 'basic forms of human good' (p. 86) (life, knowledge, play, aesthetic experience, sociability (friendship), practical reasonableness, religion) are 'all equally fundamental' (p. 92); even though 'each one, when we focus on it, can reasonably be regarded as the most important. Hence there is no objective hierarchy amongst them.' Finnis's elaboration of his model of man is subtle, learned and appealing. It would be hard to quarrel with his view that he has described forms of 'human flourishing' yearned for by human beings individually and collectively. For him, practical reasoning is to be understood as internal to a properly ordered moral-political system:

> . . . what is decisive, in discerning the content of the natural law, is one's understanding of the basic forms of (not-yet-moral) human well-being as desirable and potentially realizable ends or opportunities and thus as to-be-pursued and realized in one's action, action to which one is already beginning to direct oneself in this very act of practical understanding. (p. 45)

This involves a kind of moral-political 'faculty' which is as objectively grounded as the 'faculties' of mathematical and physical measurement and calculation: a view explicitly adopted by Aristotle, who propounded a psychological theory connecting good moral health with good moral judgement and a theory of motivation, according to which the person so endowed would be motivated by desires for things good in themselves.[100] Whether this 'to-be-pursued' gerundive *does* bridge the opposition between naturalism and anti-naturalism is questionable,[101] but I shall not pursue that question here. Instead I shall take up Finnis's idea that these 'forms of human flourishing', while 'equally fundamental', are also capable of radically different orderings by individuals:

> . . . each one of us can reasonably *choose* to treat one or some of the values as of more importance in *his* life. A scholar chooses to dedicate himself to the pursuit of knowledge, and thus gives its demands priority, to a greater or lesser degree (and perhaps for a whole lifetime), over the friendships, the worship, the games, the art and beauty that he might otherwise enjoy. (p. 93)

An individual can also *reorder* his priorities during his lifetime,[102] making a

> . . . change in his chosen life-plan. That chosen plan *made* truth more important and fundamental for him. His new choice changes the status of that value *for him*; the change is in him.

The ability of individuals to make radical conversions in their life-plans does not, for Finnis, affect the objective status of the basic values, 'the rank of intrinsic value between the basic values' (p. 94). The suggestion is that a good (objectively good) social order would promote the flourishing of all the enumerated forms of good, and that within that order it would be possible for each individual to move freely, ordering and reordering 'the status of [each] value *for him*' (p. 93). But how could such an idea apply to concrete social orders? Returning to the theme of the opposition between *Gemeinschaft* and *Gesellschaft*, it could be argued that successfully ordered exemplars of each type would embody Finnis's basic forms of good, but with a radically different ordering of the forms in each case: most importantly between the value of sociability, 'peace and harmony among men' (p. 88) and the value of practical reasonableness, 'being able to bring one's own intelligence to bear effectively . . . on the problems of choosing one's actions and life-style and shaping one's own character'. In a society where one of these two forms was sytematically fostered over the other, whether intentionally or not, an individual or group which opted to promote the other form could be systematically frustrated: hence the problems of individualistic dissidents in *Gemeinschaften* and of communitarians in *Gesellschaften*. In this sense, Finnis's adaptable 'catholicism' may have led him to underestimate the fundamental opposition between different forms of life. For although he acknowledges that within an individual one form of good may be fostered only at the expense of another, he is less willing to admit this at the level of society as a whole.[103] Yet the society which opts for consensus, security and harmony as its primary values must frustrate competitiveness, individualism, adventurousness in 'experiments of living'. Herein lies the difference in emphasis between Finnis's approach and my own: what for him is a relatively minor detail of an individual's value-scheme is for me the central problem of how to envisage the *Rechtsstaat*.

The difference between our two approaches can be developed by considering Finnis's own discussion of 'the modern usage of rights-talk' (p. 221), as it has evolved since the seventeenth century. Finnis is sensitive to the fact that 'modern usage' is specific in a number of respects: in particular it is 'modern', compared to the classical Thomist conception of *jus* as 'the just situation or arrangement', in that it makes central the claims and immunities of individuals. But, from the perspective of this book, it is also historically specific in that it forms a central part of a particular kind of social order, one in which the citizens are familiar with the mechanics of asserting rights and making and contesting claims, are prepared to invoke constitutional guarantees of their rights and live their day-to-day lives within that *Rechtsstaat* framework. Can such an order embody at the level of society as a whole the *Gemeinschaft* values of *Zusammenwesen*? That seems implausible.[104] Can it make room for them and guarantee the conditions for them to flourish at the micro-level, the level of 'experiments of living'? It can, but only if the specific conditions of the Millian libertarian order are fulfilled and those conditions exclude the promotion of certain other values, indeed, historically, can be achieved only by the sacrifice of those values, at the level of society as a whole. A *Rechtsstaat,* while remaining a *Rechtsstaat,* cannot have as its fundamental goal the promotion of love or religion. But it, and perhaps it alone, can provide an ordered framework within which these and many other goals can be pursued in a multiplicity of experiments of living. But (and this is the crucial difference between my and Finnis's positions) to live within a relatively closed, *gemeinschaftlich*-ordered group within such an open, *gesellschaftlich* society is not the same as to live within a *gemeinschaftlich*-ordered society. If the argument of this book is correct, the passage from *Gemeinschaft* to *Gesellschaft* of society as a whole is a real one, not to be transcended in the synthesis of a new higher *Gemeinschaft.* Such a transcendence would in reality be a reverse, achievable, if at all, only by force.

I am unwilling, therefore, to seek a naturalistic foundation of the *Rechtsstaat,* understood as a whole form of life, in so far as I am sceptical that any philosophical anthropology could be both general and specific enough to bridge the fact/value distinction through specifications of a shared insight into forms of human flourishing. I am also to this extent an irrationalist, in that I do not believe that a choice between experiments of living is determined by wholly rational criteria or that there should even be a set of criteria shared by all members of a pluralist society. They need only share a commitment to the principle of substantive freedom within the coercive framework of the law. But it should be noted that a commitment to the political principle of libertarian pluralism does not presuppose that philosophical position, which is positivist and non-objectivist. A high rationalist like Habermas, a philosophical anthropologist like Finnis and an objectivist like J. S. Mill may all share that commitment. Each of these may consistently argue that we should foster, as a primary value, freedom of experimentation, including freedom for error as well as for truth, while maintaining from his particular standpoint substantive criteria for evaluating whole forms of life not available to the positivist. To examine fully the logic and the history of the connection between the political principle and the philosophical position it would be necessary to write another book.[105]

NOTES

1. I. Berlin, *Two Concepts of Liberty*, pp. 14–15.
2. J.S. Mill, *On Liberty*, p. 127.
3. Ibid., p. 193.
4. Ibid., p. 128.
5. Ibid., pp. 234, 235.
6. I. Berlin, *Two Concepts of Liberty*, pp. 14–15.
7. S.E. Finer, *Five Constitutions*, 1979, pp. 25–6. But the vagueness of the wording of other articles, in particular Article 21, has allowed the *Grundgesetz* to be used for blatantly undemocratic purposes, such as the banning of the Communist Party (see R. Beddard, *Human Rights and Europe*, p. 127, for the European Commission's timidity on this question) and the enforcement of *Berufsverbot* (see G. Smith, *Democracy in Western Germany*, pp. 202–9, for the history of this practice, and for the interpretation of the *Grundgesetz* which permits it.)
8. Ibid., pp. 84–6.
9. For the vulnerability of civil rights in Britain see P. Hewitt, *The Abuse of Power*, p. 243, and the discussion of privacy on pp. 42–8, and of freedom of information in chapter 4 of her book. See also J. Michael, *the Politics of Secrecy, passim*. These topics will be discussed in section 3 below.
10. J.S. Mill, *On Liberty*, p. 193.
11. The theme of E.P. Thompson, *Whigs and Hunters*, 1975.
12. See in particular H.L.A. Hart, 'Positivism and the separation of law and morals'.
13. H. Kelsen, *General Theory of Law and the State*, 1973 edition, p. 46. The formulation of the *Pure Theory* (§17) is, in contrast, hypothetical and oblique, inviting us to examine how it is that we relate to each other in 'human behaviour':

    If we analyze our statements about human behavior, however, we discover that we connect acts of human behavior towards each other and toward other facts not only according to the principle of causality (i.e. as cause and effect), but also according to a principle entirely

> different from that of causality – a principle for which science does not as yet have a generally accepted word. (p. 76)

14. M. Hollis, *Models of Man*, 1977, pp. 118–120.
15. Page references in the text of this section are to H.L.A. Hart, *The Concept of Law*. My reading of Hart has been clarified by discussions with Angus Ross, for whose many constructive criticisms I am grateful.
16. In a number of passages, Hart explicitly dissociated his account of the internal point of view from any psychological overtones.

> The internal aspect of rules is often misrepresented as a mere matter of 'feelings' in contrast to externally observable physical behaviour. No doubt, where rules are generally accepted by a social group and generally supported by social criticism and pressure for conformity, individuals may often have psychological experiences analogous to those of restriction or compulsion. When they say they 'feel bound' to behave in certain ways they may indeed refer to these experiences. But such feelings are neither necessary nor sufficient for the existence of 'binding' rules. (*The Concept of Law*, p. 56)

(Cf. J.W. Harris, 'Olivecrona on law and language', 1981, p. 529). Hart was right to deny that the 'acceptance' of a constitutional order should be identified with or reduced to any particular set of *feelings* on the part of citizens. But this does not mean that 'acceptance' should be wholly divorced from attitudes and forms of behaviour expressing endorsement. As Hart himself went on to say:

> What is necessary is that there should be a critical reflective attitude to certain patterns of behaviour as a common standard, and that this should display itself in criticism (including self-criticism), demands for conformity, and in acknowledgments that such criticism and demands are justified, all of which find their characteristic expression in the normative terminology of 'ought', 'must', and 'should', 'right' and 'wrong'. (ibid.)

17. See Kelsen's famous comments on the 'anarchist professor of law' (*Pure Theory*, p. 218) and Harris's exposition in J.W. Harris, *Legal Philosophies*, 1980, p. 70.
18. N. MacCormick, *Legal Reasoning and Legal Theory*, 1978, p. 291.
19. Though the polarity of even that question might turn out to be less clear cut, given the presence of politically committed

acceptance by officials amongst its criteria of identity. In other words, even the presence or absence of a legal system might turn out to be a matter of degree (*a fortiori* the presence or absence of a *Rechtsstaat*). Attachment to polar oppositions is not, of course, restricted to positivists in jurisprudence. As Finnis has acutely observed, it is fundamental to the practice of law, from the most concrete piece of solicitor's advice to Supreme Court judgements of constitutionality. It is a necessary component of 'the enterprise of legal order', since the lawyer's task is to 'read off a definite solution to definite problems – in the final analysis, judgment for one party rather than the other in a litigable dispute'. J. Finnis, *Natural Law and Natural Rights*, p. 279. Equally, in constitutional cases a law is found to be valid or invalid.

20. Page references in the text in this section are to L. Althusser, *Lenin and Philosophy and Other Essays*, 1971.
21. The unstated contrasting role of ideology in the classless society is not easy to envisage on this model: in the mode of ideology (i.e. subjectivity) the individual would still, presumably, live relations that were imaginary, not scientific , but his asserted autonomy would, perhaps, no longer be illusory. It is, of course, true that Althusser's aim was to dismantle the Enlightenment component of traditional Marxist ideology theory, the cognitive theme of ideology as false consciousness, whether peddled by 'priests and despots' from without or secreted in the day-to-day operation of the production process from within. But to shift from the conception of ideology as false consciousness to that of ideology as relations lived in the imaginary mode is simply to re-locate cognitive questions within the context of that imaginary mode. Althusser did indeed repeatedly suggest that, within class relations, these imaginary relations are cognitively deceptive. L. Althusser, *For Marx*, p. 234; *Lenin and Philosophy*, p. 157. (This is the nub of Giddens's criticism of Althusser's conception of ideology in *Central Problems*, 1979, pp. 179–181).
22. How far the internal point of view either is popularly adopted or deserves to be depends on the particular history and provisions of the particular legal order. See E.P. Thompson on the freedoms embodied in the English legal system and G. Napolitano on the Italian Communist Party's role in formulating the 1948 Italian Constitution and in continuing to endorse it. (*The Italian Road to Socialism*, 1977, pp. 17–18). There are further statements on the role of the Italian Consti-

tution by E. Berlinguer and P. Ingrao in D. Sassoon (ed.), *The Italian Communists Speak for Themselves*, 1978, pp. 72–3 and pp. 191–2.

23. Habermas's account of the 'ideal speech situation' can be accepted independently of his contentious views of truth. According to one reading of his theory, the truth of utterances concerning the social world is to be *identified* with the rational consensus. The suggestion of 'rationalist totalitarianism' in that reading is hard to avoid, since truth is contained in a circle which cannot be broken by reference to a domain over against the social whole (a reference which realist philosophies of science and correspondence theories of truth attempt to maintain). Thus departure from the rational consensus can have no 'external' rational justification. But it is anyway not clear that that reading is correct. Against it, Philip Pettit has argued that Habermas tied truth to rational consensus 'non-analytically' (p secures rational consensus because p is true), rather than 'analytically' (p is true in so far as p secures rational consensus) (P. Pettit, 'Habermas on truth and justice', 1982, p. 213). Whatever the correct reading of Habermas's truth theory is, my own position is closer to Mill's more modest faith that political and social freedom are connected with the search for truth just because freedom includes the freedom to reach false as well as true conclusions and assert false as well as true propositions, and that scientific progress depends on the public guarantee of freedom of information and expression. Equally, it remains an open question whether Habermas has identified power relations with forms of distorted communication, as Giddens suggests, or whether, as I should read him, he has merely asserted that power relations are always mediated through forms of communication, from which they acquire their enduring structured form, beyond the momentary operation of force (the passage from the struggle-to-the-death to the master and slave in Hegel's *Phenomenology*). (See J. Habermas, 'Toward a theory of communicative competence', pp. 372, 374, and A. Giddens, *Studies in Social and Political Theory*, p. 152). For an excellent sympathetic account of Habermas's ideology critique, see R. Geuss, *The Idea of Critical Theory*, in particular pp. 59 ff. for the discussion of legitimacy in terms of the problematic notion of justified acceptance of the norm-system.
24. The only excuse for using this Germanism throughout the book is that the nearest English equivalent (rule of law) is already appropriated by other traditions – both natural law and

positivist – and infused by them with particular connotations. My own somewhat idiosyncratic use of the term is not intended to suggest endorsement of any particular tendency within German jurisprudence or political theory.

25. H.L.A. Hart, *The Concept of Law*, pp. 156–7.
26. H.L.A. Hart, 'Positivism and the separation of law and morals'; L.L. Fuller, 'Positivism and fidelity to law – a reply to Professor Hart', 1958.
27. L.L. Fuller, 'Positivism and fidelity to law', p. 645.
28. Ibid., p. 646. Here Fuller echoes Weber's view that questions of legitimacy are not susceptible to yes/no answers.
29. J.P. Stern, *Hitler: The Führer and The People*, pp. 116–129.
30. Ibid., p. 124.
31. Ibid., p. 126.
32. Ibid., pp. 126–7.
33. Ibid., p. 127.
34. See M. Weber, *Economy and Society*, I. pp. 215–16 for the model of 'legal authority', resting on 'rational grounds', formal, abstract and bureaucratic. See also R.M. Unger's outstanding account of the destruction of the formalist jurisprudence of the Weimar Republic in *Law in Modern Society*, pp. 216–220.
35. P. Hewitt, *The Abuse of Power*, p. 243, quoting Lord Scarman.
36. See S.E. Finer, *Five Constitutions*, pp. 77–78, where he describes the USSR constitution as a 'para-fictive constitution', and pp. 15–20 *passim* on the question 'whether constitutions matter'.
37. Constitution of the USSR (1977), Article 50 (S.E. Finer, *Five Constitutions*, p. 161).
38. H.L.A. Hart, *Concept of Law*, pp. 196–7, 201–2.
39. J.A. Lombard, *Alternatives to the Consolidation of Kwazulu* 2.3.1.
40. Ibid., 2.3.4.1.
41. Ibid., 2.3.4.3.2.
42. See J.D. Jackson, *Justice in South Africa*, 1980, *passim.*
43. *J-J. Rousseau, Social Contract,* II. p. 11.
44. N. Daniels, 'Equal liberty and unequal worth of liberty', 1975, p. 256. The European Court of Human Rights made this point explicitly in the case of Mrs. Airey: 'Mrs. Airey complained that the high costs involved to obtain the necessary legal representation before the High Court in Ireland, in seeking a judicial separation from her husband, amounted to denial of access under Article 6 (1). In agreeing with her contention and

holding a violation of the provision, the Court said:

> The Convention is intended to guarantee not rights that are theoretical or illusory but rights that are practical and effective. This is particularly so of the right of access to the courts in view of the prominent place held in a democratic society by the right to a fair trial.'
> (R. Beddard, *Human Rights and Europe*, p. 110)

45. J. Locke, *Second Treatise of Government*, §13.
46. R. Dworkin, *Taking Rights Seriously*, p. 147.
47. See Talcott Parsons, Review of Unger, *Law in Modern Society*, p. 149. The European Court of Human Rights has built Locke's condition into its definition of a 'competent court', a term which '. . . denotes bodies which exhibit "common fundamental features, of which the most important is independence of the executive and of the parties to the case" and also "the guarantee of judicial process".' (R. Beddard, *Human Rights and Europe*, p. 92). In the North of Ireland, particularly since the introduction of Diplock courtroom procedures, Locke's condition has been systematically overruled. Paddy Hillyard's work has documented the erosion of the rule of law in the province, the spread of 'unfettered ministerial discretion' as the independence of the judiciary is undermined. For his most recent account of the process, see P. Hillyard, 'Law and Order', 1983. The lack of impartial umpires to adjudicate on prisoners' complaints within Britain has been highlighted by civil rights campaigners: see P. Hewitt, *The Abuse of Power*, pp. 26–9 and G. Richardson, 'Taking prisoners' rights seriously'. The recent report by Justice, the British section of the International Commission of Jurists has recommended the appointment of an independent prisons ombudsman as part of a remedy. It has also recommended restoring certain normal civil rights to prisoners and curbing governors' disciplinary powers.
48. Some of these criticisms are noted in this chapter, particularly Griffith's wholly negative picture of the British judiciary (pp. 138 ff.) and Nonet's and Selznick's account of the shortcomings of 'autonomous law' in the USA (p. 140).
49. *Guardian*, 11 November 1980.
50. Jonathan Steele's interview with Zbigniew Bjuak, *Guardian*, 29 April 1981.
51. J. Griffith, 'Reflections on the rule of law', p. 759.
52. Ibid.
53. Though Griffith has been careful, at least in his book, to hedge

his conclusion with qualifications:

> . . . any analysis which places the judiciary in the United Kingdom in a wholly subservient position to the government misreads history and mistakes the source and nature of the common law. Those who criticize existing institutions in the United Kingdom need always to remember that, in comparison with most other countries, this country enables its citizens to live in comparative freedom. To what extent is this a consequence of our judicial system and of our judges?
>
> That they play some part is undeniable. They will even, on occasion, enforce the law which forbids arrest without reasonable cause or imprisonment without trial, and support the right of free association or, within its limits, of free speech. The idea of the rule of law is not wholly illusory. (J. Griffith, *The Politics of the Judiciary*, p. 232.)

54. Ibid., p. 238.
55. For a balanced assessment of the arguments for and against entrenchment, see Michael Zander, *A Bill of Rights?*
56. J. Griffith, *The Politics of the Judiciary*, p. 239.
57. See P. Hewitt, *The Abuse of Power*, pp. 244 ff.
58. See for example the excellent school text book complete with comprehension tests, F.G. Cullop, *The Constitution of the United States*, 1969, described on the cover as 'the great and complex document that is the backbone of the American way of life'!
59. A recent case in Utah concerns the series of tests in which

> . . . for 12 years, beginning in 1951, more than 100 atomic bombs were detonated at a test site above the Nevada desert west of here, sending huge plumes of radioactive dust and debris across the desolate red mesas and rocky buttes of southern Utah and northern Arizona.

The law suit has been

> brought by more than 1,100 current and former residents of the area who say they are suffering from leukemia or other diseases or have lost relatives to leukemia and other cancers as a result of exposure to radioactive fallout from the testing program.
>
> The suit accuses the government of negligence and carelessness in carrying out the tests and demands hundreds of millions of dollars in damages for deaths and

> illnesses suffered by nearly 300 people. (*International Herald Tribune*, 15 September 1982)

The executive's plea of 'sovereign immunity' has been challenged by the Court:

> The government believes it is covered by what is called 'sovereign immunity' – asserting that it cannot be sued for its actions because of presidential authorisation of the testing programme.
>
> Although Richard Nixon tried unsuccessfully to protect himself in a cloak of sovereign immunity at the time of Watergate, American courts have frequently accepted the plea as essential for the operation of government, so that decisions can be made without the fear of suit by private citizens. In the present case the assistant US attorney, Henry Gill, has twice called for dismissal of the charges on these grounds.
>
> However, the federal district judge, Bruce S. Jenkins, who is hearing the case without a jury, threw out both pleas because, he said, 'there are enough terribly serious questions raised in this lawsuit – not just legal issues, but social issues'. (*Sunday Times*, 21 November 1982)

60. R. Dworkin, 'Constitutional Cases' in *Taking Rights Seriously*. Dworkin uses the terms 'judicial restraint' and 'judicial activism', but shows the limits of their applicability. In a recent judgement (23 June 1983), the Supreme Court shifted its position significantly as adjudicator between the executive and legislative branches in ruling by seven votes to two 'that the legislative veto [on Presidential recommendations] introduced by Congress 50 years ago is unconstitutional' (*Guardian*, 24 June 1983). The effects of that judgement have yet to be assessed.
61. P. Nonet and P. Selznick, *Law and Society in Transition*, p. 70.
62. Ibid., pp. 63, 66, 68–9.
63. R. Beddard, *Human Rights and Europe*, p. 29. Cf. J. Griffith, *The Politics of the Judiciary*, pp. 238–9.
64. P. Hewitt, *The Abuse of Power*, p. 244.
65. R. Beddard, *Human Rights and Europe*, pp. 203–4.
66. Ibid., p. 86.
67. P. Hewitt, *The Abuse of Power*, p. 44.
68. Characteristically, Lord Denning's view of a new Bill of Rights was that it 'would encourage troublemakers' (M. Zander, *A Bill of Rights?*, p. 68).

69. The value of a relatively independent judiciary even in the grossly distorted South African system has been demonstrated by an important recent judgement:

    Tens of thousands of black migrant workers stand to benefit from one of the most important judgments ever delivered by South Africa's highest court. Earlier this week it struck down one of the central pillars of the country's pass laws, ruling that the government is no longer entitled to deny them the right to live permanently in the 'white' cities and towns.

    The historic decision, handed down by the Appellate Division of the Supreme Court, which is the country's final court of appeal, constitutes a great embarrassment for the government.

    The Appellate Division dismissed with costs the appeal by the government against a decision of a lower court. The decision means that the administration of the pass laws must be greatly liberalised at a time when the government is attempting to enforce them more rigorously than ever before. If the government now resorts to legislation to overturn the appeal judgment, it will undermine the reformist image it is so assiduously trying to promote for itself. (*Guardian*, 1 June 1983)

70. J. Plamenatz, *German Marxism and Russian Communism*, 1954, p. 138.
71. As has been amply demonstrated by the work of the NCCL. See in particular P. Hewitt, *The Abuse of Power* p. 43 and p. 88 on privacy; p. 106 on secrecy.
72. On privacy, A.R. Miller's 'Personal privacy in the computer age', 1969, is still the classic monograph, containing a vast amount of data on the implications of information technology for the law prior to the US Federal Privacy Act of 1974. A good general overview is provided by P. Stein and P. Shand, *Legal Values in Western Society,* chapter 8. For recent developments in the United Kingdom, see P. Hewitt, *The Abuse of Power,* chapter 12. C. Fried, in his paper 'Privacy', has attempted to give a general philosophical foundation of its value. On freedom of information, see P. Hewitt, *The Abuse of Power,* chapter 4 and J. Michael, *The Politics of Secrecy, passim.*
73. Quoted by S.D. Warren and L.D. Brandeis, 'The right to privacy', 1890, p. 195.
74. J. Michael, *The Politics of Secrecy*, pp. 131, 139.
75. Ibid., p. 139.

76. A.R. Miller, 'Personal privacy in the computer age', pp. 1174, 1175.
77. J. Michael, *The Politics of Secrecy*, p. 139.
78. P. Hewitt, *The Abuse of Power*, p. 43.
79. Ibid., p. 106. For an account of some of those studies, see J. Michael, *The Politics of Secrecy*, chapter 10.
80. Ibid., p. 128.
81. Ibid., pp. 129, 178.
82. A.R. Miller, 'Personal privacy in the computer age', p. 1194.
83. See J. Michael, *The Politics of Secrecy*, pp. 124–5.
84. Michael's account of developments in the United States since 1974 suggests that while 'the two Acts overlap, they do not quite mesh'. But he indicates that the fault has been in loose drafting, rather than direct conflict between the two, so that 'to be on the safe side, requests to see personal files are usually made under both Acts in order to take advantage of the favourable provisions of each'. (J. Michael, *The Politics of Secrecy*, p. 138).
85. A.R. Miller, 'Personal privacy in the computer age', p. 1107.
86. C. Fried, 'Privacy', p. 477.
87. Ibid., pp. 480 ff.
88. Ibid., p. 487.
89. Thus Stein's and Shand's criticism of Fried seems to miss the nerve of his argument: 'To the extent that in some societies privacy is valued only in a symbolic form, which is irrelevant to personal relationships, Fried's theory lacks universal validity' (P. Stein and P. Shand, *Legal Values in Western Society*, p. 193).
90. J. Finnis, *Natural Law and Natural Rights*, p. 225.
91. This in no way plays down the importance of Finnis's right. The demand for freedom of information evidently includes the citizen's 'right not to be positively lied to', a right which is flouted more or less flagrantly by many governments.
92. My distinction between real models and utopian models is similar to Bernard Williams's distinction between 'real options' and 'notional options'. For Williams, a new 'system of belief' (S2) constitutes a 'real option' for a group when it is possible for its members to 'go over to' S2 from their present system of belief (S1). That possibility depends on two conditions: 'first that it is possible for them to live within, or hold, S2 and retain their hold on reality, and, second, to the extent that rational comparison between S2 and their present outlook is possible, they could acknowledge their transition to S2 in the light of

such comparison'. (B. Williams, 'The truth in relativism', 1981, p. 139).

93. See above, section 3.3. By 'material' in this context I mean roughly what Marx meant by it. I am referring not to any position in metaphysics or philosophy of mind (mind/body determinism, identity, etc.) but to a thesis within social philosophy concerning the presence of structural–relational conditions of, and also constraints on, agency.
94. Cf. B. Williams, 'The Truth in Relativism', p. 140.
95. C. Taylor, 'Rationality', 1982, p. 94.
96. Cf. B. Williams, 'The Truth in Relativism', p. 143. It is interesting to note that many of Williams's insights were anticipated by Stephen Toulmin, *An Examination of the Place of Reason in Ethics,* 1950, pp. 152–3.
97. B. Williams, 'Conflicts of values', 1979, p. 227.
98. I follow Sartre in thinking that the model of reversal between figure and ground (the *Gestalt* switch) illuminates changes in individuals' and groups' value systems at points where the traditional rationality discussion fails to. (See in particular the *Being and Nothingness* discussions of bad faith at I.2 and of freedom at IV.1). But I do not think that that model need entail either the individualism or the voluntarism which then tempted Sartre.
99. Remaining page references in the text are to J. Finnis, *Natural Law and Natural Rights.*
100. . . . that which is in truth an object of wish is an object of wish to the good man, while any chance thing may be so to the bad man, as in the case of bodies also the things that are in truth wholesome are wholesome for bodies which are in good condition, while for those that are diseased other things are wholesome – or bitter or sweet or hot or heavy, and so on; since the good man judges each class of things rightly, and in each the truth appears to him. For each state of character has its own ideas of the noble and the pleasant, and perhaps the good man differs from others most by seeing the truth in each class of things, being as it were the norm and measure of them. (Aristotle, *Nichomachean Ethics,* 3.4.4 (113a, pp. 25 ff)
101. Toulmin had arrived at some conclusions similar to Finnis in S. Toulmin, *An Examination of the Place of Reason in Ethics,* where he too discussed 'gerundive concepts' (pp. 70–72), designed to play a similar bridging role to that of Finnis.

102. This passage is remarkably reminiscent of the early Sartre, both in its individualism (its bracketing, at least for the moment, of all social determinants) and for its voluntarism: the idea that an individual steers and gives meaning to his life by a fundamental project, which he can change during the course of his life by a radical conversion.
103. Of course, Finnis is too fine and subtle a philosopher ever to leave himself entirely without defence against the critic. Thus he acknowledges that there may be 'even very "peculiar" conventions, norms, institutions, and orders of preference, such as the aristocratic code of honour that demands direct attacks on life in duelling' (p. 91), but these, he thinks, 'we can analytically unravel' in terms of different, and perhaps bizarre, orderings of the basic goods. The parenthetical nature of this comment suggests that the problem is a relatively peripheral one for Finnis.
104. The kind of 'evidence' relevant here is questionable. Applying Finnis's principle of 'practical reasonableness' to family relations, we could argue that within the family, fairness and predictability of behaviour are a necessary component of the *Zusammenwesen,* but that *Zusammenwesen* does not seem to be able to survive the transformation – as children become adult and economically independent and parents socially and emotionally distanced from one another – of the family into a collection of individuals asserting and contesting rights, expecting the performance of specific duties from one another. This is compatible with Mill's idea of a structured pluralist order, which would make room for units not ordered as *Rechtsstaaten* within it. It is also compatible with the anthropological datum that the family in a kinship society is highly *gesellschaftlich* in regulating exchange, reciprocity, contract, etc. (regulations enforced in 'advanced' societies by private law).
105. See R. Nozick, *Anarchy, State and Utopia*, 1974, chapter 10. That chapter is a particularly interesting essay on the nature of free, contractually entered *Gemeinschaften* and the contrast between them and traditional *Gemeinschaften*. My difference with Nozick concerns the conditions for realizing libertarianism rather than the content of a libertarian society. As a pluralist, in other words, I am not committed to Nozick's principle of minimal, non-interventionist government. If it is correct that both Rousseau's condition and Locke's condition must be met if pluralism is to be a reality, not a sham, then a high level of public control of the economy will be a condition

of genuine pluralism, not an obstacle to it. For views closer to my own on these matters, see J. Mackie, *Ethics: Inventing Right and Wrong*, and B. Williams, *Moral Luck*.

Bibliography

Adams, J.C., and Barile, P., *The Government of Republican Italy*, Boston: Houghton Mifflin Company, 1972.

Adkins, A.W.H., *Merit and Responsibility*, Oxford: Clarendon Press, 1960.

Allott, A., *The Limits of Law*, London: Butterworths, 1980.

Althusser, L., *For Marx*, tr. B. Brewster, London: Allen Lane, 1969.

Althusser, L., *Lenin and Philosophy and Other Essays*, tr. B. Brewster, London: New Left Books, 1971.

Arendt, H., *On Violence*, New York: Harcourt, Brace, World, 1969.

Aristotle, *Nicomachean Ethics*, tr. H. Rackham, London: Heinemann (Loeb Classical Library), 1926.

Arthur, C., 'Towards a materialist theory of law' (1977) 7 *Critique*.

Bankowski, Z., and Mungham, G., *Images of Law*, London: Routledge and Kegan Paul, 1976.

Beddard, R., *Human Rights and Europe*, London: Sweet and Maxwell, 1980.

Bentham, J., *Constitutional Code*, vol. I (eds. F. Rosen and J.H. Burns), Oxford: Clarendon Press, 1983. First published 1830.

Berlin, I., *Two Concepts of Liberty*, Oxford: Clarendon Press, 1958.

Bromley, P.M., *Family Law* (6th edition), London: Butterworths, 1981.

Burke, E., *Reflections on the Revolution in France* (ed. Conor Cruise O'Brien), Harmondsworth: Penguin, 1969. First published 1790.

Cain, M., 'The main themes of Marx' and Engels' sociology of law' (1974) 1 *British Journal of Law and Society*.

Cain, M., Review of Z. Bankowski and G. Mungham. *Images of Law* (1976) 3 *British Journal of Law and Society*.

Cohen, G.A., 'Marx's dialectic of labor' (1974) 3.3 *Philosophy and Public Affairs.*

Cohen, G.A., *Karl Marx's Theory of History: a Defence,* Oxford: Clarendon Press, 1978.

Cullop, F.G., *The Constitution of the United States: an Introduction,* New York: New American Library, 1969.

Daniels, N., 'Equal liberty and equal worth of liberty' in N. Daniels (ed.), *Reading Rawls,* Oxford: Blackwell, 1975.

Denning, Lord, *What Next in the Law,* London: Butterworths, 1982.

Devlin, Lord Patrick, 'Morals and the criminal law' in R. Dworkin (ed.), *The Philosophy of Law,* London: Oxford University Press, 1977. From *the Enforcement of Morals,* London: Oxford University Press, 1965.

Dias, J.W., *Jurisprudence,* London: Butterworths, 1970.

Douglas, M., *Purity and Danger: an Analysis of Concepts of Pollution and Taboo,* Harmondsworth: Penguin, 1970. First published 1966.

Dworkin, R., *Taking Rights Seriously,* London: Duckworth, 1977.

Edelman, B., *Ownership of the Image: Elements for a Marxist Theory of Law,* tr. E. Kingdom, London: Routledge and Kegan Paul, 1979.

Engels, F., *Anti-Dühring: Herr Eugen Dühring's Revolution in Science,* Moscow: Foreign Language Publishing House, 1962. *Werke,* vol. 20, published 1878. (abbreviated to *AD*)

Finer, S.E. (ed.), *Five Constitutions,* Harmondsworth: Penguin, 1979.

Finnis, J., *Natural Law and Natural Rights,* Oxford: Claren don Press, 1980.

Fried, C., 'Privacy' (1968) 77 *The Yale Law Journal.*

Fuller, L.L., 'Positivism and fidelity to law – a reply to Professor Hart' (1958) 71 *Harvard Law Review.*

Geuss, R., *The Idea of Critical Theory: Habermas and the Frankfurt School,* Cambridge: Cambridge University Press, 1981.

Giddens, A., *Studies in Social and Political Theory,* London: Hutchinson, 1977.

Giddens, A., *Central Problems in Social Theory,* London: Macmillan, 1979.

Glazer, N., 'Individual rights against group rights' in E. Kamenka and A.E.S. Tay (eds.), *Human Rights*, London: Edward Arnold, 1978.

Gluckman, M. (ed.), *The Allocation of Responsibility*, Manchester: Manchester University Press, 1972.

Gramsci, A., *Selections from the Prison Notebooks of Antonio Gramsci*, ed. and tr. Q. Hoare and C. Nowell Smith, London: Lawrence and Wishart, 1971.

Griffith, J.A.G., 'Reflections on the rule of law'. *New Statesman*, 24 June 1972.

Griffith, J.A.G., *The Politics of the Judiciary*, Glasgow: Fontana, 1981.

Habermas, J., 'Towards a theory of communicative competence' (1970) 13 *Inquiry*.

Habermas, J., 'On systematically distorted communication' (1970) 13 *Inquiry*.

Harris, J.W., *Legal Philosophies*, London: Butterworths, 1980.

Harris, J.W., 'Olivecrona on law and language – the search for legal culture' (1981) 94 *Tiddskrift for Rettsvitenskap*.

Hart, H.L.A., 'Positivism and the separation of law and morals' in R.M. Dworkin (ed.), *The Philosophy of Law*, London: Oxford University Press, 1977. First published (1958) 71 *Harvard Law Review*.

Hart, H.L.A., 'Immorality and treason' in R.M. Dworkin (ed.), *The Philosophy of Law*, London: Oxford University Press, 1977. First published in *The Listener*, 30 July 1959.

Hart, H.L.A., *The Concept of Law*, London: Oxford University Press, 1961.

Hart, H.L.A., 'Negligence, *Mens Rea* and criminal responsibility' in A. Guest (ed.), *Oxford Essays in Jurisprudence* (First Series), Oxford: Clarendon Press, 1961.

Hart, H.L.A., *Law, Liberty and Morality*, London: Oxford University Press, 1963.

Hart, H.L.A., 'Bentham on legal rights' in A.W.B. Simpson (ed.), *Oxford Essays in Jurisprudence* (Second Series), Oxford: Clarendon Press, 1973.

Hart, H.L.A., 'Between utility and rights' (1979) 79 *Columbia Law Review*.

Hart, H.L.A., Introduction to J. Bentham, *An Introduction to the Principles of Morals and Legislation,* London: Methuen, 1982.

Hegel, G.W.F., *Phenomenology of Spirit,* tr. A.V. Miller, Oxford: Clarendon Press, 1977. First German edition 1807.

Hegel, G.W.F., *Philosophy of Nature* (Part 2 of the *Encyclopaedia of the Philosophical Sciences*), tr. A.V. Miller, Oxford: Clarendon Press, 1970. First German edition 1817. (abbreviated to *PN*)

Hegel, G.W.F., *Philosophy of Right,* tr. T.M. Knox, Oxford: Clarendon Press, 1942. First German edition 1821. (abbreviated to *PR*)

Hegel, G.W.F., *Philosophy of History,* tr. J. Sibree, London: Bell, 1881. First German edition 1837. (abbreviated to *PH*)

Hegel, G.W.F., *Hegel's Political Writings,* tr. T.M. Knox, Oxford: Clarendon Press, 1964. (abbreviated to *PW*)

Heiman, G., 'The sources and significance of Hegel's corporate doctrine' in Z.A. Pelczysnki (ed.), *Hegel's Political Philosophy: Problems and Perspectives,* Cambridge: Cambridge University Press, 1971.

Hewitt, P., *The Abuse of Power: Civil Liberties in the United Kingdom,* Oxford: Martin Robertson, 1982.

Hill, C., *Reformation to Industrial Revolution* (Pelican Economic History of Britain, vol. 2), Harmondsworth: Penguin, 1969.

Hillyard, P., 'Law and order' in J. Darby (ed.), *Northern Ireland: the Background to the Conflict,* Belfast: Appletree Press/New York: Syracuse University Press, 1983.

Hollis, M., *Models of Man,* Cambridge: Cambridge University Press, 1977.

Honoré, A.M., 'Ownership' in A. Guest (ed.), *Oxford Essays in Jurisprudence* (First Series), Oxford: Clarendon Press, 1961.

Hook, S., *From Hegel to Marx: Studies in the Intellectual Development of Karl Marx,* Ann Arbor: University of Michigan Press, 1968.

Hunt, A., 'The politics of law and justice' (1981) 4 *Politics and Power.*

Jackson, J.D., *Justice in South Africa,* Harmondsworth: Penguin, 1980.

Jones, J.W., *The Law and Legal Theory of the Greeks,* Oxford: Clarendon Press, 1956.

Kamenka, E., and Tay, A.E.S., 'Beyond the French revolution: communist socialism and the concept of law' (1971) 21 *University of Toronto Law Journal.*

Kamenka, E., and Tay, A.E.S., 'Beyond bourgeois individualism: the contemporary crisis in law and legal ideology' in E. Kamenka and R.S. Neale (eds.), *Feudalism, Capitalism and Beyond,* Canberra: Australian National University Press, 1975.

Kamenka, E., and Tay, A.E.S., 'Social traditions, legal traditions' in E. Kamenka and A.E.S. Tay (eds.), *Law and Social Control,* London: Edward Arnold, 1980.

Kant, I., *Kant's Political Writings* (ed. H. Reiss), tr. H.B. Nisbet, Cambridge: Cambridge University Press, 1971.

Kant, I., *On History* (ed. L.W. Beck), tr. L.W. Beck, R.E. Anchor and E.L. Fackenheim, Indiana/New York: Bobbs Merrill, 1963.

Kant, I., *Philosophy of Law,* tr. W. Hastie, Clifton: Augustus M. Kelley, 1974.

Kant, I., *The Moral Law (Groundwork of the Metaphysic of Morals*), tr. H.J. Paton, London: Hutchinson, 1965.

Kant, I., *Rechtslehre* (*Die Metaphysik der Sitten,* Erster Theil) in *Werke,* vol. 6, Berlin: Walter de Gruyter & Co., 1968. First published 1797.

Keat, R., 'Liberal rights and socialism' in K. Graham (ed.), *Contemporary Political Philosophy: Radical Studies,* Cambridge: Cambridge University Press, 1982.

Keat, R., 'Individualism and community in socialist thought' in J. Mepham and D–H. Ruben (eds.), *Issues in Marxist Philosophy,* vol. 4, Brighton: Harvester Press, 1981.

Kelsen, H., *General Theory of Law and the State,* tr. A. Wedberg, New York: Russell and Russell, 1973. Translation first published by Harvard University Press, 1945.

Kelsen, H., *The Pure Theory of Law,* tr. M. Knight, Berkeley/Los Angeles/London: University of California Press, 1967.

Koenigsberger, H.G. and Mosse, G.L., *Europe in the XVI Century,* London: Longman, 1971.

Kolakowski, L., 'The myth of human self-identity' in L. Kolakowski and S. Hampshire (eds.), *The Socialist Idea: a Reappraisal*, London: Quartet, 1977.

Lichtheim, G., 'The concept of ideology' (1965) 4 *History and Theory*.

Lloyd, D., *The Idea of Law*, Harmondsworth: Penguin, 1973.

Locke, J., *Two Treatises of Government* (ed. P. Laslett), New York/Toronto: New American Library, 1965.

Lombard, J.A. (ed.), 'Alternatives to the consolidation of Kwazulu: Progress Report', Pretoria: Bureau for Economic Policy and Analysis, University of Pretoria, 1980.

Lukács, G., *History and Class Consciousness*, tr. R. Livingstone, London: Merlin Press, 1971.

Lukes, S., 'Marxism, morality and justice' in G.H.R. Parkinson (ed.), *Marx and Marxisms*, Cambridge: Cambridge University Press, 1982.

McCloskey, H.J., *J.S. Mill: a Critical Study*, London: Macmillan, 1971.

MacCormick, N., 'Rights in legislation' in P.M.S. Hacker and J. Raz (eds.), *Law, Morality and Society* (Essays in Honour of H.L.A. Hart), Oxford: Clarendon Press, 1977.

MacCormick, N., *Legal Reasoning and Legal Theory*, Oxford: Clarendon Press, 1978.

Mackie, J.L., *Ethics, Inventing Right and Wrong*, Harmondsworth: Penguin, 1977.

McMurtry, J., 'Making sense of economic determinism' (1973) 3.2 *Canadian Journal of Philosophy*.

Maine, Sir Henry, *Ancient Law*, London: Dent, 1965. First edition 1861.

Marcuse, H., *Reason and Revolution*, London: Routledge and Kegal Paul, 1969. First published 1941.

Marx, K., *Die Frühschriften* (ed. S. Landshut), Stuttgart: Alfred Kröner Verlag, 1971. (abbreviated to Kröner)

Marx, K., *Grundrisse*, tr. M. Nicolaus, Harmondsworth: Penguin Books, 1973. *Grundrisse der politischen ökonomie*, Berlin: Dietz Verlag, 1953. Written 1857–8. (abbreviated to *G*)

Marx, K., *Capital*, volume I, tr. S. Moore and E. Aveling, London: Lawrence and Wishart, 1970. *Werke*, vol. 23; this translation is of the third German edition, 1883.

First published 1867. (abbreviated to *Cap. I*)

Marx, K., and Engels, F., *Werke,* Berlin: Dietz Verlag, 1956 ff. (abbreviated to *W,* cited by volume and page)

Marx, K., and Engels, F., *Collected Works,* London: Lawrence and Wishart, 1975 ff. (abbreviated to *CW,* cited by volume and page)

Marx, K., and Engels, F., *Marx–Engels Selected Works in One Volume,* London: Lawrence and Wishart, 1968. (abbreviated to *MESW*)

Michael, J., *The Politics of Secrecy,* Harmondsworth: Penguin, 1982.

Mill, J.S., *Utilitarianism, On Liberty* etc. (ed. M. Warnock), Glasgow: Fontana, 1962.

Mill, J.S., *Autobiography,* London: Oxford University Press, 1971.

Miller, A.R., 'Personal privacy in the computer age: the challenge of a new technology in an information-oriented society' (1969) 67 *Michigan Law Review.*

Moore, S.F., 'Legal liability and evolutionary interpretation: some aspects of strict liability, self-help and collective responsibility' in M. Gluckman (ed.), *The Allocation of Responsibility,* Manchester: Manchester University Press, 1972.

Napolitano, G., *The Italian Road to Socialism,* Interview with E. Hobsbawm, tr. J. Cammett and V. De Grazia, London: Journeyman Press, 1977.

Nonet, P., and Selznick, P., *Law and Society in Translation: Toward Responsive Law,* New York: Harper and Row, 1978.

Nozick, R., *Anarchy, State and Utopia,* Oxford: Blackwell, 1974.

O'Hagan, T., 'Rousseau: conservative or revolutionary? A critique of Levi-Strauss' (1978) 11 *Critique of Anthropology.*

O'Hagan, T., 'On the "withering-away" of the superstructures' in D–H. Ruben and J. Mepham, (eds.), *Issues in Marxist Philosophy,* vol. 4, Brighton: Harvester Press, 1981.

Parsons, T., 'Some afterthoughts on *Gemeinschaft* and *Gesellschaft*' in W.J. Cahnman (ed.), *Ferdinand Tönnies: a New*

Evaluation, Essays and Documents, Leiden: E.J. Brill, 1973.

Parsons, T., Review of R.M. Unger, *Law in Modern Society* (1977) 12 *Law and Society Review*.

Pashukanis, E.B., *General Theory of Law and Marxism*, tr. H.W. Babb, in H.W. Babb (ed.), *Soviet Legal Philosophy* (XX Century Legal Philosophy Series, no. 5), Cambridge, Mass: Harvard University Press, 1951. First published 1924.

Pettit, P., 'Habermas on truth and justice' in G.H.R. Parkinson (ed.), *Marx and Marxisms*, Cambridge: Cambridge University Press, 1982.

Pirenne, H., *Economic and Social History of Medieval Europe*, tr. I.E. Clegg, New York: Harcourt, Brace, 1937.

Plamenatz, J., *German Marxism and Russian Communism*, London: Longman, 1954.

Rawls, J., *A Theory of Justice*, London: Oxford University Press, 1972.

Richardson, G., 'Taking prisoners' rights seriously' (forthcoming)

Rousseau, J–J., *The Social Contract and Discourses*, tr. G.D.H. Cole, revised J.H. Brumfitt and J.C. Hall, London: Dent, 1973.

Ste. Croix, G.E.M. de, *The Class Struggle in the Ancient Greek World*, London: Duckworth, 1981.

Salmond, J.W., *Jurisprudence* (12th edition revised by P.W. Fitzgerald), London: Sweet and Maxwell, 1960.

Sartre, J–P., *Being and Nothingness*, tr. Hazel Barnes, London: Methuen, 1958. First French edition 1943.

Sartre, J–P., *Critique of Dialectical Reason*, tr. A. Sheridan-Smith, London: New Left Books, 1976. First French edition 1960.

Sassoon, D. (ed.), *The Italian Communists Speak for Themselves*, Nottingham: Spokesman, 1978.

Schlesinger, R., *Soviet Legal Theory*, London: Kegan Paul, Trench, Trubner, 1945.

Sharlet, R., 'Pashukanis and the withering away of law in the USSR' in S. Fitzgerald (ed.), *Cultural Revolution in Russia (1928–31)*, Bloomington: Indiana University Press, 1978.

Sheleff, L.S., 'From restitutive law to repressive law: Durkheim's *The Division of Labor in Society* revisited' (1975) 16 *European Journal of Sociology*.

Siedentop, L., 'Two liberal traditions' in A. Ryan (ed.), *The Idea of Freedom: Essays in Honour of Isaiah Berlin*, Oxford: Oxford University Press, 1979.

Simmonds, K.P. (ed.), *European Community Treaties*, London: Sweet and Maxwell, 1972.

Smith, G., *Democracy in Western Germany*, London: Heinemann, 1979.

Starobinski, J., *Jean-Jacques Rousseau: la transparence et l'obstacle*, Paris: Gallimard, 1976. First published 1971.

Stein, P., and Shand, P., *Legal Values in Western Society*, Edinburgh: Edinburgh University Press, 1974.

Stern, J.P., *Hitler: the Führer and the People*, Glasgow: Fontana/Collins, 1975.

Suter, J–F., 'Burke, Hegel and the French Revolution' in Z. Pelczynski (ed.), *Hegel's Political Philosophy: Problems and Perspectives*, Cambridge: Cambridge University Press, 1971.

Taylor, C., 'Rationality' in M. Hollis and S. Lukes (eds.), *Rationality and Relativism*, Oxford: Basil Blackwell, 1982.

Thompson, E.P., *Whigs and Hunters: the Origin of the Black Act*, London: Allen Lane, 1975.

Thompson, E.P., *Writing by Candlelight*, London: Merlin, 1980.

Tönnies, F., *Community and Association (Gemeinschaft und Gesellschaft)*, tr. C.P. Loomis, London: Routledge and Kegal Paul, 1955.

Tönnies, F., *Gemeinschaft und Gesellschaft*, Darmstadt: Wissenschaftliche Buchgesellschaft, 1969. First published 1887.

Tönnies, F., *Einführung in die Soziologie*, Stuttgart: Ferdinand Enke Verlag, 1965.

Tönnies, F., *On Sociology: Pure, Applied and Empirical*, (Selected Writings, eds. W.J. Cahnmann and R. Heberle), Chicago: University of Chicago Press, 1971.

Toulmin, S., *An Examination of the Place of Reason in Ethics*, Cambridge: Cambridge University Press, 1950.

Trilling, L., *Sincerity and Authenticity*, London: Oxford University Press, 1972.

Unger, R.M., *Knowledge and Politics*, New York: Free Press, 1975.

Unger, R.M., *Law in Modern Society*, New York: Free Press, 1976.

Vlachos, G., *La Pensée Politique de Kant*, Paris: Presses Universitaires de France, 1962.

Walker, D.J., and Redman, M.J., *Racial Discrimination*, London: Shaw and Sons, 1977.

Warren, S.D., and Brandeis, L.D., 'The right to privacy' (1890) 4.5 *Harvard Law Review*.

Weber, M., *The Agrarian Sociology of Ancient Civilizations*, tr. R.I. Frank, London: New Left Books, 1976.

Weber, M., *Economy and Society: an Outline of Interpretive Sociology* (eds. G. Roth and C. Wittith) New York: Bedminster Press, 1968.

Wesolowski, W., 'Marx's theory of class domination' in N. Lobkowicz (ed.), *Marx and the Western World*, Notre Dame/London: Notre Dame University Press, 1967.

Williams, B. (ed.), *Report of the Committee on Obscenity and Film Censorship* (Home Office) Cmnd. 7772, London: HMSO, 1979.

Williams, B., *Morality*, Cambridge: Cambridge University Press, 1976. First published 1972.

Williams, B., 'Conflicts of values' in A. Ryan (ed.), *The Idea of Freedom: Essays in Honour of Isaiah Berlin*, Oxford: Oxford University Press, 1979.

Williams, B., 'The truth in relativism' in *Moral Luck*, Cambridge: Cambridge University Press, 1981.

Winch, P., *The Idea of a Social Science and its Relation to Philosophy*, London: Routledge and Kegan Paul, 1971. First published 1958.

Young, E., 'Developing a system of administrative law?' in P. Robson and P. Watchman (eds.), *Justice Lord Denning and the Constitution*, Westmead: Gower, 1981.

Zander, M., *A Bill of Rights?*, Chichester and London: Barry Rose, 1979.

Index of Names

Adams, J.C. 82
Adkins, A.W.H. 63
Allott, A. 24–7
Althusser, L. 127–9
Arendt, H. 96
Aristotle 154
Arthur, C. 98

Bankowski, Z. 6–11
Barile, P., *see* Adams, J.C.
Beddard, R. 1, 12, 28, 157, 162
Bentham, J. 23–4
Berlin, I. 2, 99, 116–20
Berlinguer, E. 160
Brandeis, L.D., *see* Warren, S.D.
Bromley, P.M. 114
Burke, E. 21–3

Cain, M. 6
Chandelle, J-M. vii
Cohen, G.A. 70, 76–81, 85
Cullop, F.G. 163

Daniels, N. 161
Denning, Lord 21–4
Devlin, Lord 111–13, 138
Dias, J.W.M. 83–4
Douglas, M. 115
Dworkin, R. 1–2, 28, 29, 30, 81, 115, 136, 141

Edelman, B. 44
Engels, F. 45, 51–81 *passim* (see especially 54, 55, 67, 72–3)

Finer, S.E. 157, 161
Finnis, J. 102, 153–6, 159–60
Fried, C. 149, 165
Fuller, L.L. 131–2

Geuss, R. 160
Giddens, A. 159
Glazer, N. 29
Gluckman, M. 24
Gramsci, A. 45
Griffith, J.A.G. 29, 138–40

Habermas, J. 129–30, 156
Harris, J.W. 158
Hart, H.L.A. 1, 12–6, 84, 98, 99, 110, 121–7, 131, 134
Hegel, G.W.F. 2, 23, 35–43, 53, 70, 74–81, 107, 160
Heiman, G. 45, 82
Hewitt, P. 1, 21, 142, 146, 157, 161, 166
Hill, C. 44, 82–3
Hillyard, P. 162
Hollis, M. 122–3
Honoré, A.M. 44, 45, 58–60, 62
Hook, S. 82
Hunt, A. 6

Ingrao, P. 160

Jackson, J.D. 161
Jones, J.W. 61

Kamenka, E. 2, 93–6, 108
Kant, I. 2, 31–5, 37, 107, 112

Keat, R. 47–8
Kelsen, H. 122–5
Koenigsberger, H.G. 83
Kolakowski, L. 47

Lichtheim, G. 71
Lloyd, D. 13, 83, 84
Locke, J. 81, 135–7, 143–5, 147, 168
Lombard, J.A. 161
Lukács, G. 10
Lukes, S. 81

McCloskey, M.J. 102
MacCormick, N. 98, 126
Mackie, J. 169
McMurtry, J. 84
Maine, Sir H. 55–6
Marcuse, H. 42
Marx, K. 2, 45, 46–81 *passim*, 111, 127–9, 140, 143–4, 151, 167
Michael, J. 51, 79–81, 157, 165, 166
Mill, J.S. 2, 99–111 *passim*, 116–20, 149–50, 156, 168
Miller, A.R. 147–8, 165, 166
Moore, S.F. 24, 63, 82
Mungham, G., *see* Bankowski, Z.

Napolitano, G. 159
Nonet, P. 11, 18–21, 141
Nozick, R. 102, 168–9

O'Hagan, T. 30, 84

Parsons, T. 12, 98, 162
Pashukanis, E.B. 2, 62–3, 90–3
Pettit, P. 160
Pirenne, H. 78–9
Plamenatz, J. 143–4

Rankin, N. vii
Rawls, J. 26
Redman, M.J., *see* Walker, D.J.
Richardson, G. 162
Ross, A. 158
Rousseau, J-J. 32, 135–6, 143, 147, 168

Ste. Croix, G.E.M. de 84
Salmond, J.W. 63, 84
Sartre, J-P. 10, 167, 168
Scarman, Lord 29, 140, 161
Schlesinger, R. 92–3
Selznick, P., *see* Nonet, P.
Shand, P., *see* Stein, P.
Sharlet, R. 98
Sheleff, L.S. 29–30
Siedentop, L. 44
Smith, G. 157
Starobinski, J. 28
Stein, P. 52, 165, 166
Stern, J.P. 132
Suter, J-F. 29

Tay, A.E.S., *see* Kamenka, E.
Taylor, C. 115, 152
Thompson, E.P. 24, 28, 119, 157
Tönnies, F. 2, 4, 28, 86–90, 93–4
Toulmin, S. 167
Trilling, L. 46

Unger, R.M. 11–18, 72, 82, 161

Vlachos, G. 44

Wade, Lord 140
Walker, D.J. 114
Warren, S.D. 165
Weber, M. 1, 82, 122, 124, 161
Wellmer, A. vii

Wesolowski, W. 84
Williams, B. 99, 109–11, 115, 152–3, 166
Winch, P. 121–2, 124
Wolfenden, Sir John 99, 111–12
Young, E. 1, 29
Zander, M. 29, 163